I COULD HAVE BEEN A CONTENDER

---

or The Other Book of Lists

By **MARGARET OBERMAN**
& DOUG STECKLER

AVON
PUBLISHERS OF BARD, CAMELOT AND DISCUS BOOKS

This is a work of humor. The references to famous personalities are intended to be in jest, and the authors sincerely hope they will be accepted as such. Except for famous personalities, all names are fictitious and any resemblance to actual persons, living or dead, is purely coincidental.

I COULD HAVE BEEN A CONTENDER OR The Other Book of Lists is an original publication of Avon Books. This work has never before appeared in book form.

AVON BOOKS
A division of
The Hearst Corporation
959 Eighth Avenue
New York, New York 10019
Copyright © 1979 by Margaret Oberman and Douglas Steckler
Published by arrangement with the authors.
Library of Congress Catalog Card Number: 79-51389
ISBN: 0-380-46383-0

First Avon Printing, September, 1979

AVON TRADEMARK REG. U.S. PAT. OFF AND IN OTHER COUNTRIES, MARCA REGISTRADA, HECHO EN U.S.A.

Printed in U.S.A.

For Ronnie O
Love
M.G.O.

For Punkinetta
Love
D.S.

ACKNOWLEDGMENTS

We offer our thanks to the following people, for many and varied reasons.

Special thanks to Mary Emery, Dick Blasucci, Harold Ramis, Joan Scott, Susie Brietner, Susan Moldow, Mona and Dick Schaefer, Pancho and Lucy Casado, Mary DiBlosi, Olivia La Bouff, Joseph Grieco, Wayne's roommate, Anne Green, Thomas La Bouff, Mary Spencer, Ross Lawrence, Doc Lee, Wayne Knutson, Freddie Laker, James Grieco, Annette Grieco, Lorna and Doug Steckler, Marty and Augusta Oberman, and Lee M. Grieco, who was one of the world's greatest laughers.

We would also like to thank the night operator on the suicide hotline, the people who are going to throw an autograph party for us at B. Dalton Pickwick, the author of *Black Like Me* for giving us an idea, Sheriff John, and of course the Academy.

THE AUTHORS

*"If it weren't for the inquisition,
this book would be a lot more interesting."*

Miguel Cervantes

CONTENTS

4. THERE IS NO BIRTH OF CONSCIOUSNESS WITHOUT PAIN

5. EVERYBODY'S GOT ONE...A JOB

6. ALMOST...OUTSIDE THE LAW

Things People Do at a Stoplight...3 Conversations Between Policemen at a Luncheonette...4 Ways to Identify an Old Draft Dodger...1 Man Convicted of Murder with a Name Like a Cigar

7. STUDIO 54...WHERE ARE YOU?

3 Unclaimed Items in the Studio 54 Lost and Found...3 Disadvantages of Living in New York...4 Ways to Tell If the Prices Are Too High in a Restaurant...5 Ways Current American Writers Live Out 1930s Fantasy Lives...5 Early-Warning Signs That the Party Is Going to Be Boring...3 Reasons ABC Took Away Geraldo Rivera's Expense Account...4 Rational Comebacks to Use When Your Son Tells You He's Gay

8. WAY OUT WEST

1 Cowboy Who Hated His Mother...6 Subtle Ways a Couple Lets You Know They Belong to the Sierra Club...7 Things Surfers Have to Watch Out for...3 Ways West Coast Bank Tellers Personalize Their Windows...6 Things a Rodeo Star Doesn't Remember...1 Beverly Hills Matron Who Doesn't Carry a Signature Bag...5 Good Ways to Be Pretentious at a Small Dinner Party...6 Things Found in a Roadside Desert Museum...11 Unfinished Hollywood Biographies...4 Excuses Actors Use for Living in Encino, California...6 Ways to Spot an L.A. Kinda Guy...4 Dead Giveaways That You Are Attending a Real Hollywood Party...6 Ways to Tell a Trendy Restaurateur...3 Ways to Tell Runaways in Beverly Hills

9. OH WHAT A TRIP I'M ON

3 Things Not to Do When You're Stoned...5 Ways to Tell If Your Housekeeper Is Skimming Your Booze...3 Hotels to Stay Away from in Europe...4 Things Not to Do While High on Quaaludes...5 Cheap Nicknames for Fingers...3 Ways to Tell If You've Scored Primo Coke...4 Surefire Ways to Tell If You're an Alcoholic...3 Ways to Tell If Your Wife Is Dating an Analyst on the Sly...4 Things Not to Say at an AA Meeting...3 Party Favors from Gertrude Stein's Salon...4 Things Not to Say to a Junkie on a Bad Trip...3 Ways to Keep Occupied during a Turbulent Flight

10. A CHANCE TO REALLY MAKE SOMETHING OF MYSELF

7 Things Marines Do on Leave...5 Requirements of a High-Fashion Model...3 Things Overheard in the Unemployment Office...9 Things Hotel Night Clerks Do in Their Spare Time...3 Suicide Notes from Professional People...4 Ways to Tell If a Student Is Majoring in Animal Husbandry...5 Full-time Occupations for Moonlighting Cab Driv-

ers…8 Strategic Moves Executives Make to Get Higher on the Corporate Ladder…7 Things to Look for in a Handyman…9 Ways a Male Nurse Asserts Himself…7 Trade Schools to Think Twice about…7 Inventions That Never Got off the Drawing Board

11. MAY I HAVE THE ENVELOPE, PLEASE?

Clint Eastwood's 2 Favorite Facial Expressions…6 Theme Shows Merv Griffin Hasn't Done Yet…3 People You Wouldn't Want to Run into in a Dark Alley…10 Names for Horror Movies AIP Hasn't Optioned…3 Ways to Tell If a Nightclub Is a Firetrap…4 One-Man Shows to Stay Away from…1 Outfit That Looks Good with a Bow Tie…7 Main Topics of Conversation on a Slow *Tonight* Show…8 Entries from the Tule, Greenland, Film Festival…3 Mia Farrow Movies That Were Never Made…4 Celebrity Answering-Machine Messages…3 Third World Women Marlon Brando Is Not Attracted to…1 Episode of *I Love Lucy* in Which Ricky Didn't Sing "Cuban Pete"…13 Television Pilots That Never Went to Series…Henry Winkler's 5 Favorite Greetings…3 People with Eyes at Half-Mast…4 Ways Howard Hughes Spent His Golden Years…1 Actress Who Was Named after Days-of-the-Week Underwear and a Metal-Merging System…5 Theme Shows Tom Snyder Hasn't Done Yet…3 Popular Entertainers Who Shouldn't Have Fired Their Interpreters…9 Cheap Actor's Quotes…4 Exposés *Sixty Minutes* Hasn't Done Yet…5 Ways the Waltons Sign Off in Italy…8 Things Screenwriters Do When They're Not Busy Taking Drugs…3 People Who Sat through an Entire Visconti Film

12. YOU CAN'T LIVE WITH 'EM…YOU CAN'T LIVE WITHOUT 'EM

12 Things Found in a Bachelor Apartment…5 Things a Girl Must Pack on Her Honeymoon Night…9 Ways Irish Guys Like to Jock It Up on the Weekend…6 Ways to Tell If Your Girlfriend's Got Latin Blood…10 Stories Women Make Up at the Return Desk of a Department Store…5 Ways Guys Work Up a Sweat at the Y…3 Things for a Woman Not to Do during Her Time of the Month…5 Reasons Why Women Resort to Babushkas…3 Ways a Woman Can Undress Sexily Wearing Knee-High Stockings…8 Things That Make a Woman Look Older…7 Ways Jewish Guys Jock It Up on the Weekend…4 Things Not to Say to a Fellow Who Is Losing His Hair…3 Ways to Tell If a Middle-Aged Matron Was Once a Tart…7 Things a Guy Must Pack on His Honeymoon Night…6 Cute Little Ways Italian Men Say "I Love You"…7 Prerequisites for a Jewish-American Princess

13. YE LITTLE ONES

3 Reasons Not to Have Children…6 Prerequisites for a Summer-

Camp Counselor...4 Ways to Tell If Your Son Is Flunking Out of College...6 Names for Children of the Late '60s...4 Things Boy Scouts Should Watch Out for...4 Things Girl Scouts Should Watch Out for...3 Alternatives to Day-Care Centers...3 Entertainers Who Weren't Blacklisted in the Fifties...3 Excuses to Give to Get out of Gym Class...5 Ways to Tell If a Child Is Abused...3 Things John Boy Never Said to His Parents...3 Entries from 14-Year-Old Debbie Mullens' Diary...7 Remarks Teachers Love to Write on Test Papers...4 Things to Keep on Hand for the Babysitter...5 Ways to Keep Your Daughter from Marrying an Ethnic Minority...5 Toys Your Parents Wouldn't Buy for You When You Were a Kid...10 Things Air Force Brats Do in Their Spare Time...6 Things Your Kids Do That Make You Wonder If There Was a Mix-up at the Maternity Hospital...5 True Lies Your Mother Told You

14. 80 YEARS YOUNG

10 Behavioral Tips for Attending a Nursing-Home Dance...5 Things a Sexagenarian Widower Does in His Spare Time...5 Gifts for a Mobile-Home Warming...7 Things Blue-Haired Ladies Talk about at Matinees...3 Wealthy Felines Who Died and Left Their Fortunes to People...14 Events at the 1980 Special Senior Citizens' Olympics...1 Thing a Mexican Man over Sixty-Five Is Called...3 Things That Make It Difficult to Give Mouth-to-Mouth Resuscitation...5 Things to Look for in a Funeral Plot...5 Alternative Careers for George Jessel...11 Requirements for Thrift-Shop Employees

15. I COULD HAVE BEEN A CONTENDER

3 Occupations Popular with Ex-Prizefighters...3 Celebrities Who Studied Acting with Eliot Janeway...8 Lines of Conversation Overheard While Waiting in Line for Hockey Tickets...5 Things Guys Look for in a Bookie...3 People Not to Take on a Ride through the Tunnel of Love...3 Ways to Spot a Former Dust Bowl Refugee...6 Things Security Guards Do with Their Spare Time

16. TAKE ME TO YOUR LEADER

4 First-Person Accounts of a UFO Sighting in Topeka, Kansas...4 Ways to Spot a Phony Psychic...6 Sympathetic Things to Say to Air-Heads...6 Favorite Overlooked Sights...3 Last Resorts after You've Tried EST, TM, Scientology, and Esalen...3 Things Chubs Do When They're Alone in a Public Restroom...10 Things S.F. Freaks Do in Their Spare Time

17. POLITICIANS AND BEAUTICIANS

9 of Jerry Brown's Favorite Zen Sayings...3 Phrases Most Often

Heard in a Beauty Salon...3 Mexican-Americans Who Do Not Own Velvet JFK Rugs...3 of Idi Amin's Favorite Hobbies...3 Ways to Tell If a Political Cartoonist Has Gone Stale...3 of Bella Abzug's Favorite Substitutes for Hats...1 Macrobiotic Name for a Governor's Sister...4 Testimonials for Arbuckle Weight-Loss Products...7 Superstitions Popular among Police Chiefs...5 Things Not to Say to the Wife When She Comes Home from the Beauty Salon

18. NONE DARE CALL IT NEWS

9 Headlines the *National Enquirer* Took a Pass on...4 Classified Apartment Ads to Stay Away from...5 Ways Greta Garbo Spends Her Saturday Mornings...3 Excerpts from Henna Renz's Gossip Column...3 Mimeographed WASP Christmas Letters...12 Signs of the Undiscovered Zodiac and Their Forecast for the Month of June—Any Year...5 Familiar Explanations Given to Claims Adjusters...7 Hints Héloïse Didn't Take Seriously...13 Questions and Answers from TV Mail Call

19. I CAN NAME THAT TUNE IN THREE NOTES

3 Ways Bob Dylan Warms Up for a Concert...6 Things Record Executives Do in Their Spare Time...1 DJ Not into Polyester...3 Reasons the Beatles Will Never Get Back Together...5 Hip Ways to Get Noticed at a Rock Concert...1 Man with a Name Like a Sincere Bathroom Fixture...4 Catch Phrases of Stereo-Component Salesmen...4 Ways to Tell a True Music Lover...8 Things Found in Bruce Springsteen's Overnight Bag...3 Non-Blacks Named after Precious Stones...3 People Who Claim to Be Former Pips...3 Catch Phrases Frequently Used by a Cocktail Pianist...6 Jobs for the Rockettes Once They Finally Close Radio City Music Hall...3 Pop Singers Sammy Davis Hasn't Claimed As a Brother

20. ALL THE NUTS AREN'T IN THE NUT HOUSE

7 Things Found in the Personal-Effects File at Bellevue Hospital...6 Excuses Matchmakers Give When the Match Goes Adrift...3 Media Princesses Who Think That Gucci Is a Sign of the Zodiac...4 Things a Man Does to Let You Know That He Is a Preppie at Heart...6 Popular Swedish Suicides...5 Ways to Spot a Circus Performer on the Street...3 of Joe Don Baker's Alternative Choices for First Name...4 Ways You Let a Friend Take Advantage of You...6 Prerequisites for Working in an Art Gallery...4 Situations Where You Should Ask for ID

21. ILLITERATI

6 Things Found in Ernest Hemingway's Overnight Bag...5 Un-

common Bumper Stickers...1 Person Who Didn't Read *Fear of Flying*...5 Ways Zelda Got on F. Scott Fitzgerald's Nerves...3 Obscure Literary Anecdotes...3 of the Longest Sentences Ever Written Excerpted from Very Obscure '40s Detective Novels...3 *Playbill* Biographies from the Hit Musical Comedy *Heat Rash*...6 Cheap Quotes Found in Week-at-Glance Diaries...8 Self-Help Books in Search of Publishers...5 Victorian Novels Overlooked by the *New York Times Book Review*...6 Want Ads You Are Likely to Find in an East Coast Literary Magazine...3 Excerpts from "Revealing" Biographies

22. THEOLOGY

4 Ways to Get a Jehovah's Witness off Your Back...10 Ways Parish Priests Raise Extra Money...6 Patron Saints Removed from the Calendar...4 Requirements Needed to Join the Jesuits...5 Snappy Retorts to Discourage an Overzealous Hare Krishna...3 Ways the Pope Spends His Day Off

1
FRESH OFF THE BOAT

15 Ethnic Groups and Their Favorite Businesses to Go Into

1. Armenians: gas-station proprietors.
2. Albanians: improvisational actors.
3. Italians: Las Vegas air-conditioning repair.
4. Argentinians: altar-boy-discipline service.
5. Orientals: Camaro-decorating service.
6. Belgians: French-seam inspectors.
7. Appalachian White Trash: welfare consultants.
8. Wasps: paint-by-number canvas restorers.
9. Jews: troubleshooters.
10. Puerto Ricans: pest bronzing.
11. Druids: ecclesiastical camp wear.
12. Gypsies: mobile-home spotters.
13. Swedes: centerfold outfitters.
14. Lebanese: rhinoplasty removers.
15. Samoans: character assassination.

3 Ways Orientals Slow Down While Driving

1. Dragging their Zorries.
2. Having engine trouble with the Camaro.
3. Scouting for crabgrass.

7 Specialties in a Wasp Delicatessen

1. Cream of mushroom soup on anything.
2. Chocolate-covered cherries.

3. Burgers and milk.
4. Soft-boiled eggs.
5. Tuna-and-potato-chip casserole.
6. Ribs (prime).
7. Salad bars.

4 WAYS ARAB WOMEN TRY TO WESTERNIZE THEMSELVES

1. Wearing woolen chaps.
2. Jaywalking.
3. Learning all the verses to "Dixie."
4. Using Aqua Filters.

3 THINGS POLISH-AMERICANS DO TO GET OUT OF WORK

1. Quit.
2. Sign up for chemotherapy treatments.
3. Put the finger on the munitions directors of the PLO.

3 WAYS GAS STATION ATTENDANTS SHOW 'EM WHO'S BOSS

1. Unplugging the pop cooler.
2. Waiting for their theatrical agent to call.
3. Playing chicken on their grease dollies.

7 COME-ONS TO A MEXICAN WAITRESS

1. "What's a nice *sēnorita* like you doing in a *casa* like this?"

2. "Your skin is like *leche*."
3. "The *dos* of us could make beautiful music together."
4. "If you've got the *dinero*, I've got the *tiempo*."
5. "*Gracias* to you, I'm in love."
6. "Hey, what's the matter, *gato* got your tongue?"
7. "I'm just *loco* about you."

3 FEARS OF JAPANESE GARDENERS

1. Tall dogs.
2. Somebody knocking off their pith-helmet connection.
3. Killer bees.

3 WAYS TO TELL IF A PERSON IS REALLY FRENCH

1. The nicotine stains on his nose.
2. He wears see-through socks.
3. He takes his Saturday-night bath once a month.

5 MOST VALUABLE POSSESSIONS OF AN ITALIAN-AMERICAN

1. The stigmata of St. Anthony on his baby finger.
2. His Jerry Vale records.
3. His mother's parole papers.
4. His ex-wife's hospital bills.
5. His "I Am a Jamoke" button.

7 THINGS ITALIAN-AMERICAN INTERIOR DECORATORS GET A DISCOUNT ON

1. Plastic covers.
2. Plaster-of-paris statues of Michelangelo's *David*.

3. Pressboard room dividers.
4. Electric water grottoes.
5. Wax fruit.
6. Red velvet drapes.
7. Floor-to-ceiling table lamps.

6 TIP-OFFS THAT YOU ARE
ATTENDING AN ITALIAN WEDDING

1. If the word "svelte" doesn't apply to any of the women in the wedding party.
2. If the bride's father threatens to put his new son-in-law's head through the photographer.
3. If the priest is wearing alligator shoes.
4. If the maid of honor is six months along.
5. If the bride is wearing a coin changer.
6. If more than half of the wedding guests know who Vic Damone is currently married to.

8 MOST COMMON FEARS OF LOW-RIDERS

1. Having their Angora dice shed.
2. A malfunction in their hydraulic lifters.
3. Making sure their rear deck speakers are visible enough.
4. Starch in their T-shirts.
5. Not finding an undersized steering-wheel cover.
6. Not being able to fit a six-pack in their console.
7. Mascara stains on the back seat.
8. Finding Cuban heelmarks on the dashboard.

3 GHETTO KITCHEN AIDS

1. No ice-cube trays.
2. A tripe shovel.
3. The Colonel.

1 LEADING SOURCE OF INCOMING BUSBOYS INTO THE U.S.

1. San Juan, Puerto Rico.

3 THANK-YOU NOTES FROM TWILA RUBELLA CLEVELAND'S WEDDING

1. Dear Moselle and Cassius,

   Sorry you could not attend the nuptials.

   We thank you for the his and hers Lucite platform shoes with the live goldfish in the heels. (I told Grover he should have fed his.)

   As soon as Grover gets his disability check, we'll be goin' to see his mama in Detroit. She done got a bad case of the blues. Whitey left her again, and her brand-new vinyl sectional was repoed.

   > Still your sugar smack,
   > Twila Rubella Cleveland

2. Dear Kareem and Sugar,

   Thank you for the out-of-sight one-size-fits-all dashiki made by Virgo Exports. Grover gets it during the week and I get it on weekends.

   Whoee! How 'bout that reception? Sorry we ran out of Pepsi.

   You two will have to come over to the pad as soon as Grover's cousins are apprehended.

   > Sail on,
   > Twila Rubella Cleveland

3. Dear Leon and Leola,

   Thanks for the lava lamp; it hit the spot. Grover has eaten up the entire bottle of passion pills you gave us, but I don't see

5

a difference, although he says his hairline has stopped receding.

And a special thanks to you, Leona, for doing my corn rows for the wedding.

Your lovin' niece,
Twila Rubella Cleveland

2
I'D LIKE TO SEE THE MANAGER

3 EARLY-WARNING SIGNS THAT THE LANDLORD IS GOING TO RAISE THE RENT

1. He starts kvetching about the tax situation.
2. He leaves a basket of avocados on your doorstep.
3. He asks you if you want to put your dogs in the pool.

9 THINGS SUPERMARKET CASHIERS DO IN THEIR SPARE TIME

1. They practice phrenology by examining honeydew melons.
2. They scrutinize an 8x10 glossy of Ruth Gordon for makeup tips.
3. They complain about the fact that the *National Enquirer* hasn't done a story on Engelbert Humperdinck in the last three issues.
4. They synchronize their gum popping to the tunes on the radio.
5. They Scotch-tape their spit curls to their cheeks.
6. They get divorced.
7. They try to find a pair of really sheer support hose (with tummy tamer).
8. They look around for their other earring.
9. They try to decide whether it's a bear market or a bull market.

7 SNAPPY RETORTS TO THE MOVING MAN

1. "Break one more thing and I'll repo your dolly."
2. "Am I paying you by the hour, or by the cigarette?"

3. "Lovely to look at, delightful to hold, if you wreck it, I mark it sold."
4. "Remember, I've got your fingerprints."
5. "Well, it *was* a stereo."
6. "What do you mean, 'So what—it's insured'?"
7. "No, I don't know a liquor store that delivers."

6 THINGS USUALLY FOUND IN A BARBERSHOP

1. Hair-covered plastic plants.
2. An 8x10 glossy of Sandy Koufax with an inscription that reads, "Dear Sam, I'll make a deal with you: I won't cut hair if you won't play baseball. Love, Sandy."
3. A Farrah Fawcett-Majors poster with Frankenstein stitches all over it.
4. A ditsy manicurist who's crazy about cats and lives alone.
5. A cat with an infected ear.
6. A sign saying, "Free Kittens."

10 WAYS TO TELL IF A HOTEL IS SLEAZY

1. The night clerk is a dead ringer for Elisha Cook, Jr.
2. The door to your room is coin-operated.
3. The bellboy wears go-go boots.
4. When "With or Without" means mosquito netting.
5. They're filming a segment of *Baretta* in the lobby.
6. There's a plaque in the elevator reading, "Sam Cooke Slept Here."
7. Each floor has its own set of stray cats.
8. There's a corn pad in the soap dish.
9. The night maid is wearing a "Do Not Disturb" button.
10. Twenty-four-hour room service means you'll get it within twenty-four hours.

6 Ways to Tell That the Postal Service Is Getting Worse

1. You get an invite to the premiere of *Birth of a Nation*.
2. You receive a sample tube of Ipana.
3. You get a post card from Atlantis.
4. You finally get a thank-you note from Bundles for Britain.
5. Your Book-of-the-Month Club selection is *Little Women*.
6. Your draft notice tells you to report to Appomattox.

6 Excerpts from the French Restaurant Guide to Skokie, Illinois

1. THE VEAL FACTORY
   396 Self-Righteous Blvd.
   PRICE RANGE: Moderate to Slightly Unreasonable
   Shuttle bus leaves every half-hour from the 10th Street FotoMat

   A charming nook tucked in the back of Woolworth's, the Veal Factory is the perfect cafeteria for either a quick lunch or a quick dinner or even a quick after-theater supper. Owner Vino Veritas is quick with a welcome and with suggestions of "best bets."

   Try the Chili Riviera or the highly spiced Carne Noir. Both are prepared with *mucho brio* by Chef Alex Jacinto (formerly with the El Adobe chain).

   The bar's a hangout for sports and opera buffs alike. Be sure to ask for the Eye Opener, three parts gin and five parts vodka with a twist...or the Shape-Up Special, eight parts neutral spirits.

   Don't miss the gift and *groceria* area where you can stock up on French foodstuffs and pottery.

2. THE COCK AND EGG
   87190 Highway 210
   PRICE RANGE: Inexpensive to Pensive

Self-parking on shoulder of Highway 210

Some Francophiles swear by the Cock and Egg; I say it's passable. The real attraction here is the bevy of topless waitresses.

A warm family restaurant with a contented clientele.

3. HOUSE OF HOLLANDAISE
7110 Retail Ave.
PRICE RANGE: Prohibitively Moderate
Parking here can be a real problem. The House of Hollandaise is in the middle of the Skokie garment district. You might try sneaking into the parking lot behind Yves' Ready-to-Wear.

Boris Hollandaise in the kitchen and son Marco behind the cash register, Mama in the ladies' room and daughter Llala behind the pastry cart...the Hollandaises impart a special foreign magic to every meal. Although a chain, the standards are highly adequate. The overall feeling is like a French sidewalk café crammed into somebody's living room.

The Bac O Bits Bouillabaisse is a must, as is the starkly robust Chicken Tartare. If you're a liver lover, don't miss the Rack of Dover Sole.

There is a small additional charge for silverware, which is only fair, since the busboys have extra work.

4. MISTER PIERRE
567 Avenue of the Snapshots
PRICE RANGE: Dirt Cheap to Very Moderate
Convenient parking across the street at O'Hare International Airport

Although technically this is not a Skokie restaurant, it is included here because of its popularity among Skokie transplants in the O'Hare area. Mister Pierre is discussed by some stewardesses in hushed tones of reverence. This is due in part to the rather large number of professional men at the bar and also the free dry-roasted peanuts.

You may bring your own children to the large, sprawling dining room, but they will be turned away, so we suggest making arrangements with Norman the Clown, who operates a rather profitable day-care center next door.

The Belgian Mules Marinade is excellent, I'm told, but I wouldn't eat mule if you paid me and since Mister Pierre is a commercial operation, that situation is unhappily, alas, reversed.

The ambience is Marseilles Garage Sale. The wine list is serviceable, as is the powder-room attendant.

5. LES FRÈRES KODIAK
5227 Judy Street
PRICE RANGE: Moderate Plus Gratuity
Validated parking with seventy-five-dollar minimum purchase

Les Frères Kodiak could be the setting for a Dan Greenburg *Esquire* article, if it were not for the floor-to-ceiling pastel murals depicting the fifty states. Racetrack fans jam the Igloo Bar, and host Karl Kodiak has memorized the odds on all the drinks. Whether you're wetting your whistle with an Anchorage Zombie or "test driving" a Nome Gimlet, don't leave the bar without dipping into the complimentary Salmon Heart hors d'oeuvres! *C'est incroyable!*

The Frog's Legs Sans Flippers are scrumptious and are quaintly served on a lily pad with a pond-scum garnish. If your taste runs this side of exotic, you'll probably find yourself ordering the Fried Breast of Chicken à la Colonel, although prepare for a forty-five-minute wait. This is a special order.

Desserts here are unfortunately limited to a rather meager selection of Trident Gum and sugarless breath mints. *Cela ne fait rien.*

The maitre d' does an excellent impression of Hayley Mills. Don't miss it!

6. TOTAL CLEAR
139½ So. Sandstone
PRICE RANGE: Whatever's Reasonable and Proper
PARKING: Wherever you want to

A former EST trainer who left the organization "while the

getting was good," host Yuron Yurone launched his all-organic restaurant in 1976. Since then, he has garnered a clientele that runs the gamut from New Wave politicians to unemployed street pharmacists.

Don't be put off by the word "organic." Yuron tells me it means "whatever's tasty and wholesome."

The specialty of the house is the Filet de Soy Bean Curd Stuffed with Alfalfa Pellets, but you'd do well to order it to go because of the stench. There's also a large dinner salad called Sprouts, Sprouts, and more Sprouts. And instead of a bread tray, there are brewer's yeast tablets to munch on throughout your meal.

Monumentally casual, the maitre d' frequently turns away garbage collectors and militant lesbians for being overdressed.

4 Ways to Tell a Man Was Once a POW

1. He's living proof of the phrase, "Shave and a haircut...two bits!"
2. He insists he started the drawstring-pants fad.
3. He refuses to eat his dinner unless it's shoved under the door.
4. When he shampoos his hair, he calls it brainwashing.

3 Ways to Get Noticed at a Poolside Resort

1. Let the air out of your neighbor's float and sing, "Slip Sliding Away."
2. Paint an FM radio band on your chest and ask if anyone wants to tune you in.
3. Lie lifelessly on the bottom of the pool a la *Sunset Boulevard*.

5 Things Health Inspectors Like to Find in Mexican Restaurants

1. 150 cockroaches in single file, swaying to the Latin rhythm of a conga drum.

2. Waitresses who must wear hairnets on their legs.
3. Rats wearing parkas in the freezer.
4. Busboys all wearing flea collars.
5. A chef who chants Miranda warnings to the food.

9 WAITRESS'S NEW YEAR'S RESOLUTIONS

1. To stop dating policemen.
2. To try not to get white shoe polish on her hose.
3. To try and remember to press her hankies.
4. To file her nails before she gets to work.
5. To get her varicose veins tied.
6. To abstain from asking her customers their astrological signs.
7. To learn how to add without using her fingers.
8. To keep the salad dressing off her hands.
9. To call a truce with the chef.

6 THINGS TO DO WITH DAY-OLD BREAD

1. Use it as spacers between your toes while doing a pedicure.
2. Cram it in your cheeks and scare the grandchildren like Brando in *The Godfather*.
3. If it's diet bread, use it as a bookmark.
4. Set it behind the furnace and start your own penicillin factory.
5. Fold a slice in half and use it as an eyeglass rest.
6. Sew it in the armpits of shirts and use it as a dress shield.

3
YOUR PLACE OR MINE

4 UNCOMMON PICK-UP SPOTS FOR SINGLES

1. The outpatient ward at the VA Hospital.
2. At the Sicilian holding tank on Ellis Island.
3. At a Sam Levinson Autograph Party.
4. In the ready-to-wear department at Firestone.

10 SWEET LITTLE THINGS FOR THE MACHO MALE TO DO ON DATES

1. Let her polish your medallions.
2. Make her go to bed with you before you take her out to dinner.
3. Ask her if she would like a nice Hawaiian Punch.
4. Have her slavishly clean your apartment and reward her by not calling her "the slut" when you introduce her to friends.
5. Keep her up to date on how much money you've spent on her.
6. Make her dress up like a French maid on Halloween.
7. Yank her princess phone out of the wall.
8. Give her cab fare after making love at your place.
9. Make her switch to a female gynecologist.
10. Force her to wear a bra under her halter top.

5 TIP-OFFS THAT A BLIND DATE IS GOING TO BE LESS THAN THE GIRL OF YOUR DREAMS

1. The address you have been given to pick her up at is the Braille Institute.

2. The only picture you've seen of her hangs in the post office.
3. Her dad works for the circus.
4. She's not into shaving.
5. When you ask her where she wants to eat, she says, "Someplace a long ways from Customs."

7 LETTERS *PENTHOUSE* WOULDN'T PRINT

1. Dear Sirs:

Two days before I was to return stateside, my teanser was blown off by a stray piece of gook shrapnel. I was awarded a twenty percent disability compensation. It's been almost eight years since the accident (accident? Who's kidding who?) and I receive forty-seven dollars a month restitution. I figure my sex life has been one hundred percent disabled and therefore deserve two hundred and thirty-five dollars a month! Either that or the Army should provide me with a live-in hooker who knows how to operate that damned prosthesis they sewed on! What do you think and can you help?

Sgt. Raymond Worney, Retired
Filter, Wyoming

2. To Whom It May Concern:

I love the odor of fresh record jackets. A friend recently caught me smelling the new Jean-Paul Rampal album and said I was real sick. Okay, I know I'm sick, but how sick am I?

Tim Nonesuch
Owatanna, WI.

3. Dear Sirs:

My fiancé slammed his manhood in the door of his Porsche 911. Does this mean I won't be able to have children?

Tina Shatto
Albuquerque, N.M.

4. Dear Sirs:

I am presently a freshman at the University of South Dakota and like all freshmen (male and female) reside in an on-campus dormitory. I guess it's to get you better orientated or something. Well, let me tell you, I am getting the education of my life!

Moulton Hall, the men's dorm where I live, is only about eighty feet from the girls' dorm, and believe you me, every night about 11:30 it is "Strip City" right across the quadrangle! You cannot imagine the gazongas on some of these babes! There's one fox who must have a pair of 45s; and does she know how to shake 'em? You bet! It's almost as though she knew someone was watching her gazongas! Well, someone is...me!

I can't speak for all the guys on my side of Moulton Hall, but I'm going to major in pre-med, 'cause when I get out, I'm going to be a gazonga specialist!

Roland Trip III
Vermillion, S.D.

5. Dear Sirs:

My husband is a big baseball fan, but he has a very small skeender. I'm wondering if there's any connection.

Jane Sahlice
Chitown, Illinois

6. To You:

I am a twenty-three-year-old blond cake model (I jump out of cakes). The head baker where I work says I should be on TV. We want to know: (A) How do I get on TV? and (B) How does a baker become a theatrical agent.

Dianne Lorch
Lexington, Kentucky

7. Dear *Penthouse*:

I would like to submit the following for consideration in your Erotic Poetry Contest:

16

I see London
I see France
I see Lulu's underpants
I am not tied down to the word "London" and if you think there is a more erotic city, I will follow your discretion.

Mitch Markowitz
Updike, Michigan

3 THINGS NOT TO SAY TO A WOMAN YOU'VE JUST MADE LOVE TO

1. "Haven't I seen you in *National Geographic?*"
2. "The smallest I have is a five."
3. "Got any cake?"

6 EARLY-WARNING SIGNS OF A BAD MARRIAGE

1. Your wife's pet name for you is "Occupant."
2. Your husband goes next door to use the john.
3. You start buying contraceptives with preservatives added.
4. Your mate signs you up for Parents Without Partners.
5. When your wife tells you she's pregnant, you reply, "Well, don't look at me."
6. One of the kids is hit by a car, and your wife says, "Nothing like this ever happened on my side of the family."

5 WAYS TO PICK UP CHICKS

1. Hang around the brooder.
2. Be nice to the mother hen.
3. Slip her some corn bits.
4. Walk like a rooster.
5. Buy some next Easter.

5 Customs to Ensure the Birth of a Male Child

1. Put a package of Pall Malls in your pillowcase.
2. Paste a picture of John Garfield to the roof of your mouth.
3. Wear straight-legged Levi's during foreplay.
4. Get Charles Bronson to autograph your wife's diaphragm.
5. Show your wife flashcards of the Washington Monument.

7 Things Hookers Should Stock Up on

1. Friends at the stationhouse.
2. Go-go-boot polish.
3. Sob stories.
4. Oysters.
5. A six-pack of Crab-No-More.
6. Thank-you notes.
7. Soap-on-a-rope.

5 Musts on a Divorce Checklist

1. Selling your side of the story to *New West* magazine.
2. Chanting your maiden name.
3. Doctoring up the family photo album.
4. Calling the local Scientology office for an estimate.
5. Looking for a loophole in the church's excommunication laws.

3 Things That Shouldn't Be Discussed the Night before the Wedding

1. Why you have to live in a mobile home.
2. His heroin habit.
3. Her mother.

7 Surefire Lines to Hook a Man with

1. "I have an independent income."
2. "I know how to snap it; it runs in my family."
3. "I'm a cocktail waitress."
4. "I'm a Scorpio."
5. "The way to a man's heart is through his shorts."
6. "The doctor says in a couple of years I may lose my voice completely."
7. "I do windows."

7 Occasions Where Houseboys Are Not Considered Proper Companions

1. Divorce court.
2. A ballgame.
3. A Parisian street café.
4. An audience with the Pope.
5. A women's caucus.
6. Your high school reunion.
7. A performance of *Uncle Tom's Cabin*.

3 Thank-You Notes from Sherry Levine Rossberg's Wedding

1. Dear Uncle Saul and Aunt Fran,
   The plastic menorah is just beautiful. David and I already have two others so now we will never be in need on the High Holidays. I always say you can never have too many menorahs, if you know what I mean. I also want to thank you for pointing out the fact that Kreeger's had my very same wedding dress on sale. My feelings weren't hurt at all. It's really important to know these things. So, thanks

again from both of us. As soon as we get the condominium decorated, we would like to have you over for brunch.

Love,
Sherry Levine Rossberg

2. Dear Shirl and Bernie,

David and I want to thank you for the ten books of trading stamps you gave us as a wedding present. The thought was so perfect, allowing us to get what we need. Too bad Bloomingdale's doesn't have a redemption center. Ha ha.

Well, anyway, Shirl, my mother told me that you felt very bad when you slipped and called David a schvartz to Uncle Irvin, and it got back to me. It's okay. He doesn't mind that even though he is only half black. It was very sweet of him to convert from Islam to Judaism, just for me. He's a real prince.

Thanks again,
Sherry Levine Rossberg

3. Dear Cousin David and Sally,

Thank you for the lovely wedding present you gave us both. Your contribution to the Jewish Defense League in our names, in lieu of a toaster, was such a unique thought. (Although I don't have a toaster.) Thanks for not calling David a schvartz. We really appreciate that.

Love and kisses,
Sherry Levine Rossberg

5 THINGS THAT PROVE CONCLUSIVELY THAT MEN EXPERIENCE A HORMONAL CYCLE

1. They burst into tears when they hear their 100% cotton imported bikini socks were lost by the laundry.
2. They refuse to go to a cocktail party because his ex brother-in-law Chuck is going to be there.

3. They won't come out of the cabana because someone made a joke about their spare tire.
4. They take the day off to go to a Fran Tarkenton autograph party.
5. They walk around the house declaring, "You think it's easy being a man?"

5 WAYS TO MAINTAIN GOOD PR AT A BROTHEL

1. Tip the guard dogs.
2. Bring plenty of nylons.
3. Save your knife tricks for the kids.
4. Compliment your companion on her "teddy."
5. Avoid saying, "Don't spend it all in one place."

4
THERE IS NO BIRTH OF CONSCIOUSNESS WITHOUT PAIN

5 Ways to Tell If a Person Is on an Emotional Rollercoaster

1. They start dating Leslie Van Houten.
2. They have a rollbar installed in the shower.
3. They think a Bob Stack is a hairdo in the shape of a chimney.
4. They start collecting Leno Ventura stills.
5. They burst into tears when they see a Ben Casey shirt.

6 Things a Psychiatrist Does to Let You Know It's Time to Change Analysts

1. When you call to apologize for missing an appointment, he says, "That's okay, I've heard it all before."
2. He keeps saying, "I think you'd be happier as a homosexual."
3. When you come in for a session, he puts on a copy of Peggy Lee singing "Is That All There Is?"
4. He slaps his forehead and says, "I'm stymied!"
5. His cure for depression is a new hat.
6. He refers to you as a Freudy Cat.

5 Lines of Small Talk to Avoid at a Black-White Wedding

1. "Do you ever watch the *Dinah* show?"
2. "Poor Dorothy Dandridge."
3. "At least half the kids will have rhythm."

4. "All I know is, I wouldn't change *my* name to Shaft."
5. "It's gotta be sexual."

10 ACRONYMS FOR NONPROFIT ORGANIZATIONS

1. C.L.A.P. — Cashiers Laugh at Pimps.
2. S.H.O.E. — Socialist Hotheads or Europeans.
3. O.U.C.H. — Out-of-towners Understand Cerebral Hemor-
rhages.
4. D.I.T.Z. — Dermatologists Initiate Test Zits.
5. C.H.E.A.P. — Children Help Entertain Asian Pups.
6. H.O.S.T.I.L.E. — House Owners Stick Taxes in Legal En-
trails.
7. W.A.C.K.Y. — Women Allow Cops Kinky Yummies.
8. D.I.P.S. — Dancers Inviting Political Struggles.
9. C.R.A.M.P.S. — Cranky Rastafarians Admitting Money
Punctuates Sales.
10. A.F.T.E.R.S.H.A.V.E. — Authors Fight Testy Entertaining
Rascals, So How About Volleyball,
Everybody?

3 PEOPLE WHO STILL USE THE WORD "NEGRO"

1. Alex Haley.
2. Leo Durocher.
3. Ed Sullivan.

5 WAYS TO TELL IF YOUR CARTIER TANK WATCH IS A PHONEY

1. You bought it from a Gypsy who was leaving the area.
2. The watchband is edible.
3. "Cartier" is spelled with a K.

4. The hands are painted on the face.
5. The numbers are written in Spanish longhand.

4 TACTFUL WAYS TO LET FRIENDS KNOW THAT THEIR PERFORMANCE AT THE COMMUNITY THEATER BOMBED

1. "I hope you didn't quit your day job."
2. "Think what you could have done with four weeks more rehearsal."
3. "It was a comedy?"
4. "Which one were you?"

3 WAYS TO SPOT A REFORMED FLOWER CHILD

1. He hangs his old Earth Shoes from his rear-view mirror.
2. When he gets a speeding ticket, he shouts, "The whole world is watching!"
3. He reads *Newsweek* under a blacklight.

5 WAYS TO KEEP THAT BLACK JOCKEY LAWN ORNAMENT IN VOGUE

1. Tell your friends you bought it at an auction sale from the estate of Uncle Ben.
2. Set a place at the table for him when the affirmative-action people come over for dinner.
3. Put a cowboy hat on him and tell everyone it's an original Remington bronze.
4. Place him on your dashboard and tell your passengers he's St. Rufus.
5. Tell them it's a valuable prop from *Cabin in the Sky*.

5 SHORTCUTS TO FINDING YOURSELF

1. Take Polaroid snapshots of your wardrobe and pore over them for color and contrast.
2. Alter all your identification the way you would like it to read.
3. Test your dog's loyalty by asking him if he wants to remain with you or move to your cousin Jack, the butcher's, house.
4. Do a Rorschach test by blotting your makeup.
5. Open a boutique at a mountain resort.

3 REASONS TO HANG ONTO THAT BLUE VELOUR JUMPSUIT

1. There's a chance you may be invited to Wayne Newton's next dress rehearsal.
2. Your wife has tentatively invited the Ink Spots over for a rib feed.
3. Next Halloween you'll be able to go trick-or-treating as Bob Crosby.

3 PERSONALITIES WHO STILL CALL WOMEN "GALS"

1. Burt Reynolds.
2. Johnny Carson.
3. Kate Millett.

10 THINGS NOT TO SAY DURING AN ENCOUNTER GROUP

1. "Now that you've got your head together, you can start on your face."
2. "All the nuts aren't in the nuthouse."
3. "If you keep listening to Janis Ian albums, you'll never get better."

4. "None of your beeswax."
5. "Now I understand why your father hung himself."
6. "Primal, schmimal, you're talking too loud."
7. "Ah, c'mon, Ethel, a breakdown is a breakdown."
8. "I just calls 'em as I sees 'em."
9. "So, if it isn't Mr. Budinski!"
10. "Well, excuse me for living."

5
EVERYBODY'S GOT ONE...A JOB

7 PROFESSIONAL MEN TO BE LEERY OF

1. Credit dentists who put in wax fillings.
2. Plastic surgeons whose specialties are eyeglasses and a mustache attached to your new nose.
3. Dieticians who serve hors d'oeuvres in the waiting room.
4. Psychiatrists who use a sleeping bag instead of a couch.
5. Bankers who tell you you must have jacks or better to open an account.
6. Radiologists who ask you if you want your X-rays borderless or with a matte finish.
7. Neurosurgeons who recommend lobotomies for menstrual cramps.

8 THINGS COCKTAIL WAITRESSES DO DURING THE DAY

1. Upper-torso exercises.
2. Count change.
3. Pencil in their eyebrows.
4. Rack their brains to remember the name of the man who slept over last night.
5. Fill out credit applications.
6. Write to Ann Landers about the problems of night blindness.
7. Enroll in a course at cosmetology school.
8. Watch reruns of the Three Stooges.

11 SPARE-TIME ACTIVITIES FOR SALESMEN AT CONVENTIONS

1. Riding mopeds through the hotel lobby.

2. Taking their joy buzzers in for their 500-mile check-up.
3. Getting their fezes blocked.
4. Short-sheeting the entire fifth floor.
5. Getting their whoopie cushions vulcanized.
6. Guessing the number of stitches in their leisure suits.
7. Stopping the elevator between floors and yelling, "Ernest Borgnine!"
8. Holding the room-service waiter hostage for more Cokes.
9. Trying the hotel chef in a kangaroo court.
10. Trying to get the busboys to give them their sisters' phone numbers.
11. Terrorizing Chinatown with noisemakers.

4 Truckdriver's New Year's Resolutions

1. To shave his back once a week.
2. To stop asking young female hitchhikers to hop in the cab and get a load of his stick shift.
3. To memorize the wife's first name.
4. To open a checking account.

7 Excuses a Comedian Gives to Rationalize No Laughs

1. The audience was drunk.
2. The audience was sober.
3. They were expecting Elvis.
4. There was a fight in the lobby.
5. They were all friends of his ex-wife's.
6. They were uncomfortable because of the leg irons.
7. Wakes are always tough.

3 Common Exaggerations from a Dental Hygienist

1. When I get through with you, you are going to have spaces that you didn't know existed.

2. When I get through with you, you are even going to hear better.
3. When I get through with you, these will look like baby teeth.

4 Things a School-Crossing Guard Thinks About While "Doing It"

1. Her fluorescent-orange ski vest.
2. A pulsating red light.
3. Thirteen-year-old Buzzy Cahack's extremely attractive buns.
4. The principal who got away.

7 Things to Omit from Your Executive Résumé

1. The time you got into the car accident and you were wearing dirty underwear.
2. That oh so expensive place where you got your eyebrows done.
3. That "waiting for the right job to come along" job.
4. The real reason why you had to have a chauffeur's license.
5. Your stage name.
6. An itinerary of the year you took off work to track down your real father.
7. A photo of you and the rest of the boys on the chain gang.

8 Ways Ballet Dancers Spend Their Spare Time

1. Defecting.
2. Brushing out their hairpiece.
3. Going comparison-shopping for Pretty Feet.
4. Making sure their tutus don't get too, too.
5. Using tea cozies for leg warmers.
6. Staying out of the sun.
7. Cruising for orthopedic jeans.
8. Posing for music boxes.

3 Things Graphic Artists Do in Their Spare Time

1. Ransack their loft for a half-empty pack of French cigarettes.
2. Name their dog Pigment.
3. Call the nearest Army-Navy store and ask if they do alterations.

8 Things American Waiters Do to Try to Pretend That They Are French

1. Cultivate a good courtesy laugh.
2. Throw their hands in the air and yell "Say la vie."
3. Affect a bisexual posture.
4. Leave the table as they are taking your order to take a personal phone call.
5. Ask for their tips in francs.
6. Never miss an opportunity to present their buns to madame.
7. Insist on telling long, involved anecdotes about the wine you've just ordered.
8. Compliment your date on her chignon.

3 Phrases Popular with Realtors

1. "This room can serve as a bathroom or a den."
2. "Those aren't wasp nests; that's track lighting."
3. "Who needs heat in New Hampshire?"

A Stewardess's Big 3 New Year's Resolutions

1. To get the wheels rotated on her luggage.
2. To try and rent an apartment with only two roommates.
3. To finish reading *Charlotte's Web*.

5 Things You Can't Get at a PX

1. Courtesy.
2. Deutschmarks.
3. A live one.
4. A hot tub.
5. A panda.

4 Characteristics of a Show Biz Doctor

1. You don't make an appointment with him, you take a meeting.
2. His cure for a hooker's VD problem is Nix Chix Trix.
3. He has his surgical-glove prints in front of Grauman's Chinese Theatre.
4. When somebody says, "Is there a doctor in the house?" he stands up and takes a bow.

8 Things That Make a High School Janitor Lose His Temper

1. Somebody putting coffee in his Kahlúa.
2. That sixteen-year-old tease in Mrs. La Bouff's English class who won't give him the time of day.
3. Having the civics teacher ask him to guest-lecture on his eighteen-month stint in the pen.
4. Being asked to be the mascot for the football team.
5. Having to operate the Ferris wheel during carnival days.
6. Being in charge of the shoes at the sock hop.
7. Having to play straight man to the P.E. teachers.
8. Having to sort the gym clothes at the end of the year.

5 Things Commercial Airline Pilots Do to Relax during a Transatlantic Flight

1. Play chicken with the North Star.
2. Pull up alongside a 747 and press a ham.

3. Try to go no-hands through major turbulence.
4. Ask the stewardess if she would like to know why they call it a cockpit.
5. Put a restroom sign on the emergency exit.

3 NECESSITIES FOR A WOMAN EXECUTIVE

1. An ability to trade one-liners with limo drivers.
2. Knowing how to remove wine stains from leather pumps.
3. A high tolerance for blazer wearing.

6
ALMOST...OUTSIDE THE LAW

6 Ways to Tell If Your House or Apartment Is Being Cased

1. There's a Volvo parked in your space.
2. There are chalk marks on the baby.
3. Somebody finally drank that bottle of Ouzo.
4. There's a message for Bo Belinsky on your answering machine.
5. The neighbors inquire if you have relatives visiting from the "old country."
6. There are six pages missing from your first-edition copy of *Hollywood Babylon.*

5 Favorite Comments by a Bail Bondsman

1. "What do you mean your first name is Skip?"
2. "I'm going to need more of an address than 'the big house.'"
3. "Do you think I *ought* to take hats as collateral?"
4. "Manson is not my idea of a family name."
5. "May I have your autograph?"

3 Indications Your Relations with Your Daughter-in-Law Have Soured

1. She thinks in-laws are the same as outlaws.
2. Her Christmas card is addressed, "To Whom It May Concern."
3. When she hears the word "family," she switches to ABC.

5 NECESSITIES FOR A GOOD TIME IN LAS VEGAS

1. A flesh-colored magnet.
2. A matching white belt and shoes.
3. Plenty of smokes.
4. Worry beads.
5. Lots of chocolate bars to give the girls.

12 POPULAR RITUALS COMMON TO ALL HALFWAY HOUSES

1. No tipping.
2. Taking inventory of your bedbugs by votive light.
3. Hassling the social director.
4. Calling roll.
5. Insisting that your halfway-house cookies are just as good as tollhouse cookies.
6. Playing hooky during the deprogramming classes.
7. Wearing a long-sleeved shirt when you meet your parole officer.
8. Having the neighbors call you "one of the goon squad" and being proud.
9. Acting unusual.
10. Endorsing your bunkmate's welfare checks.
11. Bullshitting about the Holocaust (the night the weirdos burned the mattresses).
12. Being on twenty-four-hour call for rap sessions.

3 MOST DISGUSTING PREMIUMS GIVEN BY A SAVINGS & LOAN ASSOCIATION

1. Cookies baked by the manager's wife.
2. A hand-painted necktie (your choice of three national park scenes).
3. A mud facial given by one of the friendly tellers.

10 Ways Derelicts Spend Their Spare Time

1. Telling stories about the Crash.
2. Playing ventriloquist with their undershorts.
3. Using jumper cables for dental floss.
4. Telling fish stories about the sock that got away.
5. Ordering Sterno straight up.
6. Talking about passing the bar exam.
7. Giving each other the hotfoot to keep warm.
8. Going comparison-shopping for park benches.
9. Writing home for blankets.
10. Insisting that *Barefoot in the Park* was written about them.

5 Early-Warning Signs That Tell You It's Time to Switch Cleaners

1. There are scorch marks on the hangers.
2. Instead of getting a laundry ticket, you get a lottery ticket.
3. They use a branding iron for a laundry marker.
4. All of the clerks are dressed as croupiers.
5. When you enter, the counter clerk throws his arms around you and yells, "Ernest Borgnine!"

6 Things Convicts Do to Pass the Time on Death Row

1. Try to build up their tolerance for electricity by swallowing batteries.
2. Translating *I Want to Live* into a Southern American dialect.
3. Trading their lawyer in for a literary agent.
4. Tipping the guard to score them some Very-Quick Tan.
5. Asking the warden if they can hang around until their savings bonds mature.
6. Putting Truman Capote on hold.

8 Things to Do When a Burglar Breaks In

1. Ask him if you can take a Dramamine before he shakes you down.
2. Launch into your Blanche DuBois impression.
3. Tell him the pantyhose he's wearing takes ten years off his face.
4. Tell him the next-door neighbor has a $10,000 stereo system and free pizza.
5. Apologize to him because the house is a shambles.
6. Slip him a five and point to the dog.
7. Ask him to come back later, because you're cleaning your oven.
8. Scream *"Ernest Borgnine!"* and grab his gun.

3 Items That Are the Last to Go at a Garage Sale

1. Disposable vacuum bags.
2. Frances Faye, *Caught in the Act* albums (Vols. 1 & 2).
3. An attractive silk blouse with symmetrically balanced nursing stains.

4 Things People Do at a Stoplight

1. Count their nose hairs using the Braille system.
2. Blot their lipstick on the dashboard.
3. Do a one-minute passion play with the religious statues on the dash.
4. Try to get their five-inch platform heel unstuck from the clutch pedal.

3 Conversations Between Policemen at a Luncheonette

1. WAITRESS
   Hi, Phil. Hi, Jack...You two fellas on Code 7? What can I do you for?
   POLICEMAN PHIL
   I think I'll have the usual...and a big milk.
   POLICEMAN JACK
   Just give me a slab of that rhubarb pie and a big milk, please.
   WAITRESS
   I think we might be out of big milk. Let me check with the chef. Can I have your menus, fellas? (*Exit*)
   POLICEMAN PHIL
   She's cute.
   POLICEMAN JACK
   Yeah. Say, Phil, isn't your wife a nurse?
   POLICEMAN PHIL
   She's an LVN.
   POLICEMAN JACK
   Oh, by the way, did you hear about O'Flaherty?
   POLICEMAN PHIL
   No.

2. WAITRESS
   Hi, Bill. Hi, Todd...You two fellas on Code 7 again?
   POLICEMAN BILL
   Hell no...you must be thinking of Phil and Jack.
   POLICEMAN TODD
   Yeah, we just saw them pulling out of the parking lot.
   WAITRESS
   What have you got for dinner...a half hour?
   POLICEMAN BILL
   Forty-five minutes.
   POLICEMAN TODD
   We don't need any menus. We know what we want.
   WAITRESS
   Shoot!...Just joking, guys.
   POLICEMAN BILL AND POLICEMAN TODD
   Ha ha ha ha ha ha ha.

POLICEMAN BILL
We'll have two Papa Burgers and two big milks.
POLICEMAN TODD
Ditto.
WAITRESS
Ha ha ha ha ha ha.

3. WAITRESS
Hi, Fred, and hellooooooo, Captain Jimmy! You two boys on Code 7? What can I bring up to your table?
CAPTAIN JAMES
Can we see the menus please, dear?
WAITRESS
You got 'em, Jimbo.
CAPTAIN JAMES
What looks good to you, Fred?
POLICEMAN FRED
Well, Captain James...I think I just want a big milk.
CAPTAIN JAMES
Me, too, and...a side order of fries.
WAITRESS
No big milk. I can bring you boys an ice tea.
CAPTAIN JAMES
Okay with me. Okay with you, Fred?
POLICEMAN FRED
Okay.
WAITRESS
My pleasure. (*Exit*)
CAPTAIN JAMES
Say, Fred, isn't your wife an RN?
POLICEMAN FRED
No. She's a waitress.

4 Ways to Identify an Old Draft Dodger

1. All his business cards have charred edges.
2. When his wife wants to make love with the lights on, he asks if he can do alternative service.

3. When his barber is too busy to take him, he asks for an appeal.
4. He won't acknowledge Joan Baez' last divorce.

1 MAN CONVICTED OF MURDER WITH A NAME LIKE A CIGAR

1. Juan Corona.

7
STUDIO 54...WHERE ARE YOU?

3 UNCLAIMED ITEMS IN THE STUDIO 54 LOST AND FOUND

1. Diana Vreeland's Hotcomb.
2. Toni Tenille's Lip Cake.
3. Phyllis Newman's talk-show itinerary.

3 DISADVANTAGES OF LIVING IN NEW YORK

1. Discovering your phone number is one digit away from Dial-A-Gay.
2. Being called "Spaz" by your doorman.
3. Paying protection money to your paperboy.

4 WAYS TO TELL IF THE PRICES ARE TOO HIGH IN A RESTAURANT

1. They demand you pay a cleaning deposit on the napkins.
2. There's a cover charge to watch the owner's daughter do her homework.
3. The cashier uses a 24-karat emery board.
4. You've seen the ladies' washroom attendant on the cover of *Vogue*.

5 WAYS CURRENT AMERICAN WRITERS LIVE OUT 1930s FANTASY LIVES

1. Calling their breakfast bar the "round table."
2. Referring to their savings and loan as the Left Bank.

3. Playing computer bullfight.
4. Comparing Abigail Van Buren's and Dorothy Parker's physical characteristics.
5. Insisting that condescending is something that Condé Nast did when he didn't like someone.

5 EARLY-WARNING SIGNS THAT THE PARTY IS GOING TO BE BORING

1. There's a rumor that the Governor is going to drop by later.
2. You discover large empty Tupperware cartons in the entryway.
3. The host and hostess are wearing matching dashikis.
4. You're the only one not wearing a lobster bib.
5. Unusual bleeding or discharge.

3 REASONS ABC TOOK AWAY GERALDO RIVERA'S EXPENSE ACCOUNT

1. He ordered out Chinese for the entire country of Panama.
2. He charged three junkets to England to find out if Paul McCartney was really dead.
3. He hired a dialectician to teach him to sound ethnic.

4 RATIONAL COMEBACKS TO USE WHEN YOUR SON TELLS YOU HE IS GAY

1. "You're not going to pin this one on me."
2. "That explains the leotards."
3. "I thought you were getting a little too old for the Scouts."
4. "I suppose this means no grandchildren."

8
WAY OUT WEST

1 COWBOY WHO HATED HIS MOTHER

1. Oedipus Tex.

6 SUBTLE WAYS A COUPLE LETS YOU KNOW THEY BELONG TO THE SIERRA CLUB

1. Their dog house is done in the shape of an A-frame.
2. Their maid is an American Indian.
3. They're on a first-name basis with Eddie Bauer.
4. They think a city slicker is an in-town raincoat.
5. On Halloween they dress up Junior as Smokey Bear.
6. They think "squatters' rights" means first dibs on the bath-room.

7 THINGS SURFERS HAVE TO WATCH OUT FOR

1. Night school.
2. "Puka" itch.
3. Jacques Cousteau.
4. Hodaddies.
5. Sand in their burgers.
6. Kamikaze seagulls.
7. Winking sharks.

3 WAYS WEST COAST BANK TELLERS PERSONALIZE THEIR WINDOWS

1. With their ceramic doggie collection.

2. With a box marked "Emergency Only," containing a year's supply of nail mender.
3. With a copy of *Gum Snappers' Almanac*.

6 THINGS A RODEO STAR DOESN'T REMEMBER

1. His name.
2. That little Indian girl that gave birth to his children.
3. His stand-in work for Don Murray in *Bus Stop*.
4. The last time he went without painkillers.
5. His calling Golda Meir the sweetest little heifer this side of the Suez.
6. Hiring a gardener to take care of his boot trees.

1 BEVERLY HILLS MATRON WHO DOESN'T CARRY A SIGNATURE BAG

Not available at press time.

5 GOOD WAYS TO BE PRETENTIOUS AT A SMALL DINNER PARTY

1. Tell long anecdotal accounts of Thomas Wolfe's love affair with Aline Bernstein, and be sure not to let anyone change the subject.
2. Wear a shirt with an iron-on transfer of your master's thesis on the front.
3. Preface every statement with, "You probably wouldn't understand this, but I have a few really close comrades that would."
4. Wince when someone mentions the name of a discount department store and leave the table without excusing yourself.
5. Comb your hair with your fingers at the table.

6 THINGS FOUND IN A ROADSIDE DESERT MUSEUM

1. Stuffed blackjack dealers.
2. A roulette wheel made out of arrowheads.
3. A happily married cocktail waitress.
4. Free drinks if you keep walking through.
5. The television Elvis kicked in while he was watching Robert Goulet.
6. A broken cake of Roy Rogers Rouge.

10 UNFINISHED HOLLYWOOD BIOGRAPHIES

1. *Margaritas, Huaraches, and Cub Scout Uniforms*—the Linda Ronstadt story.
2. *Lookalikes*—half of this book is about singer Andy Williams; the other half about producer extraordinaire Robert Stigwood.
3. *If a Mule Answers*—the life of actor/dancer Donald O'Connor.
4. *I'm Still Young, I Could Still Grow*—the Steve Cauthen story.
5. *A Man Called Clotheshorse*—the real story behind George Hamilton, the man.
6. *Short-Changed and Fit to Be Tied*—a little bit about Paul Williams.
7. *I've Been Married Since Then*—the Eliott Gould story.
8. *Thank God for Residuals*—the Desi Arnaz story.
9. *I Knew Monty, but We Were Different Types*—actor Kevin McCarthy's life story.
10. *My Little Career*—the life story of Gail Storm as told to Ann Sothern.

4 EXCUSES ACTORS USE FOR LIVING IN ENCINO, CALIFORNIA

1. The Negroes in the area are all professional musicians or baseball players.

2. Nobody notices when you wear a yarmulke.
3. The Saks' in the valley has a drive-through window.
4. The city streets are named after game-show hosts.

6 Ways to Spot an L.A. Kinda Guy

1. He's the only one at a garden wedding wearing his high school gym shorts.
2. He won't buy a three-piece suit because he's against the polyester slaughter.
3. His description of Leonard Cohen is "vivacious."
4. His idea of going back east is San Bernardino.
5. He dates a black chick hoping to improve his tan.
6. He spells relief T-E-Q-U-I-L-A.

4 Dead Giveaways That You Are Attending a Real Hollywood Party

1. If the only person in the room not wearing a piece of second-hand clothing is the maid.
2. If the hostess walks around quoting Gertrude Stein.
3. If the guy you are having a meaningful conversation with turns out to be someone's limo driver.
4. If a hush falls over the room when somebody says they have found a good, cheap Mercedes mechanic.

6 Ways to Tell a Trendy Restaurateur

1. He has his first name legally changed to Chez.
2. His head busboy used to be Allan Carr's majordomo.
3. He insists that he is the illegitimate son of Mike Romanoff.
4. There's an original Cugat over the bar.
5. He's on a first-name basis with Fabian.

6. He's got a pair of James Coburn's old espadrilles in a glass case displayed in the foyer.

3 Ways to Tell Runaways in Beverly Hills

1. Their backpack is from Gucci.
2. When they get arrested they put their bail on a charge card.
3. They have their nannies do their hitchhiking for them.

9
OH WHAT A TRIP I'M ON

3 Things Not to Do When You're Stoned

1. Have a garage sale.
2. Call the police and ask them to read you the Miranda warnings.
3. Juggle steak knives.

5 Ways to Tell If Your Housekeeper Is Skimming Your Booze

1. She wears a lampshade on her head while cleaning.
2. You found her catching forty winks in the bathtub.
3. When your husband comes home she offers him a round on the house.
4. She tries to open a bottle of Windex with a corkscrew.
5. On cleaning day she arrives carrying an eight-pack of beer nuts.

3 Hotels to Stay Away from in Europe

1. Le Miserable, Paris, France.
   A delightful hovel, just around the corner from the Rue de Rude. Fourteen nooks with plenty of space under the door for room service. A favorite of those who are stuck in Paris, and have lost their traveler's checks. Le Miserable is located in the heart of the famed wallpaper district. This establishment caters to small wigs and dipsomaniacs alike. Be sure to ask to see the room that Gabby Hayes slept in.

2. The Brown Jackson, London, England
   This place is a haven for rock stars and limo chauffeurs. The hotel offers indestructible furnishings in lovely day-glow shades. Some of the luminaries that have passed through its portholes have included singing star Rhonda Linstadt, the Sir Douglas Quintet, and the Seeds. Be sure to visit the Del Close Rocket Room during your stay.
3. The Leon Spinksola, Rome, Italy
   A watering hole for prizefighters and Vegas greeters. A special added attraction is a credit dentist on the fourth floor. The Spinksola is very inconvenient to everything except the ever-popular Tony Goomba 24-hour Bail Bond Service.

4 Things Not to Do While High on Quaaludes

1. Go no-hands on a roller-coaster ride.
2. Get picked up for loitering in your living room.
3. Rearrange your filing system.
4. Try to climb into a Maxfield Parrish print.

5 Cheap Nicknames for Fingers

1. Digits.
2. Smokey links.
3. The Gabors.
4. Mother hand and her five lovely daughters.
5. The Pep Boys.

3 Ways to Tell If You've Scored Primo Coke

1. Your connection is a personal friend of Juan Valdez.

2. You start stamping DECEASED on incoming mail.
3. You try to go wing walking on your Chevy.

4 SUREFIRE WAYS TO TELL IF
YOU'RE AN ALCOHOLIC

1. You pour Jim Beam on your morning Wheaties.
2. When manicuring your nails, you keep the nail-polish remover in a shot glass.
3. When you get the DTs, you think you're watching the swallows return to Capistrano.
4. You use Johnny Walker to thicken gravy.

3 WAYS TO TELL IF YOUR WIFE IS
DATING AN ANALYST ON THE SLY

1. She demands an answer to her question, "Do you or do you not think that Andy Kaufman is a young Van Johnson?"
2. She insists you were a pirate in a former life.
3. She made her own birthday cake and topped it with the slogan, "I'm not going through the change!"

4 THINGS NOT TO SAY AT
AN AA MEETING

1. "Last call!"
2. "I'd feel more comfortable if this place had stools."
3. "I have to leave early—there's a reunion at the drunk tank."
4. "Anybody got any Sen-Sens?"

3 PARTY FAVORS FROM
GERTRUDE STEIN'S SALON

1. An 8x10 glossy of Gertrude and Alice Toklas doing the Cake Walk.

2. A 78-rpm record of Gertrude doing her Spencer Tracy impression.
3. A signed Walter Keane painting.

4 THINGS NOT TO SAY TO A JUNKIE ON A BAD TRIP

1. "Why do you need that stuff? Let's go get a diet cola."
2. "Let's go fry up a mess of sparrows!"
3. "Cheese it, the cops!"
4. "What's the matter with your teeth?"

3 WAYS TO KEEP OCCUPIED DURING A TURBULENT FLIGHT

1. Give yourself a home permanent.
2. Ask for an extra bag of peanuts.
3. Point at the stewardess and say, "It's a doozy!"

10
A CHANCE TO REALLY MAKE SOMETHING OF MYSELF

7 THINGS MARINES DO ON LEAVE

1. Try to get the name on their tattoo changed.
2. See how many guys they can cram into a four-for-a-quarter picture booth.
3. Try to act British.
4. Adjust the hem on their floodpants.
5. Go to night court as a spectator.
6. Storm the box office after seeing *Scorpio Rising*.
7. Enroll in Berlitz to study Creole.

5 REQUIREMENTS OF A HIGH-FASHION MODEL

1. Ability to look good with the mouth open.
2. Readiness to date at all times.
3. Ability to memorize Social Security number.
4. Intelligence not to judge a book by its weight.
5. Instinct to know when not to show stretch marks.

4 THINGS OVERHEARD IN THE UNEMPLOYMENT OFFICE

1. "Eef I could be speekin' the English, do you thin' I could be stand here?"
2. "Call the cops, 'cause I ain't leaving."
3. "I understand that the teller at window three used to be with the Yardbirds."
4. "Rita Moreno has promised me a definite job offer."

9 Things Hotel Night Clerks Do in Their Spare Time

1. Try to remove the keyhole imprints from their cheeks.
2. Play "Emergency Breakthrough" on the switchboard.
3. Collar the maids.
4. Order out for ice.
5. Read the guests' post cards.
6. Switch the numbers on the room keys.
7. Chant "Calling all cars!" over the PA.
8. Play "Connect the Dots" with the night maid's freckles.
9. Hide the house dick's trench coat.

3 Suicide Notes from Professional People

1. Marv Goodbar—Certified Public Accountant
   The books wouldn't balance, the auditor's coming, and I'm rejecting my hair transplant. My life has been in the red so long, the only way out is physical bankruptcy.
   I've gone over this twice and I still can't figure it.
   P.S. Please bury me on either the first or the fifteenth.

   Marv

2. Biff McCadden—Construction Worker
   A lot of lousy stuff has been happening to me lately:
   A. Somebody ran over my lunch box with a forklift.
   B. The laundry put too much starch in my favorite work shirt.
   C. My wife's hair is overdry and overbleached. I can't take it anymore and by the time you read this, I'll be forty flights down.

   Sincerely,
   Biff

3. Waldo Perkins—Theater Usher
   Why didn't my famous dad ever help?

   Junior

4 Ways to Tell If a Student Is Majoring in Animal Husbandry

1. He bought his prize heifer a friendship ring.
2. When he does something bad, he won't come out from under the table.
3. He's popular with women because he can lick his eyebrows.
4. He's the National Secretary of the Dan Haggerty Fan Club.

5 Full-time Occupations for Moonlighting Cab Drivers

1. Russian Jew.
2. Cub reporter for the *National Enquirer.*
3. Fast-facial expert for Bloomingdale's.
4. Psychic interpreter of needle tracks.
5. Coin-collection appraising.

8 Strategic Moves Executives Make to Get Higher on the Corporate Ladder

1. They start calling everyone babe.
2. They have a five-gallon decanter of Aramis on their desk.
3. They break up with their secretary.
4. They fix their boss up with a real she-woman.
5. They go into a restaurant partnership with a pro athlete.
6. They smile a lot and say, "I can live with that."
7. They break up with the receptionist.
8. They break up with the boy in the mailroom.

7 Things to Look for in a Handyman

1. A permanent address.

2. Legible references.
3. An industrial-strength sweatband.
4. Spare batteries for his transistor radio.
5. A maximum of three (3) black fingernails.
6. A low sex drive.
7. His own martini shaker.

9 WAYS A MALE NURSE ASSERTS HIMSELF

1. Talks dirty.
2. Wears a wrist corsage.
3. Brown-noses the interns.
4. Goes to real-estate school at night.
5. Frosts his hair (Betty Crocker).
6. Confuses Flo Ziegfield with Flo Nightingale.
7. Wears clogs.
8. Trades in his Nova convertible for a Trans Am.
9. Has an extra-large ass.

7 TRADE SCHOOLS TO THINK TWICE ABOUT

1. SPAZ "BERNARD" SPARTAN'S SCHOOL of SECURITY GUARDING
   Graduate Joey Baggy says, "Lasts week I didn't even knows how to spell 'security guard'...now I is one!"
2. EUGENIE GREENHENNY'S SCHOOL of JEWISH-AMERICAN ROYALTY
   "We specialize in the hard-to-place."
3. AMERICAN ACADEMY of ESCORT ART
   Graduate Joey Baggy says, "Lasts week I didn't even knows how to spell 'escort' ...now I is one!"
4. RENEE VAPIDE'S SCHOOL of DATEKEEPING
   "Our client list reads like a *Who's Who* of the modeling world....Ask about our special seminar for air-heads."
5. THE BEAVER'S SCHOOL of NEWSPAPER FOLDING
   "Leave it to Beaver!"

6. KIMBERLY NOVAK'S SCHOOL of CAREER ANCESTRY
   "We trace your mistakes."
7. LORD NIGEL'S GRAMMAR ACADEMY
   Graduate Joey Baggy declares, "It matters not that only one week ago I had no concept of 'grammarian'…now I is one!"

7 Inventions That Never Got off the Drawing Board

1. Spot remover for Dalmatians.
2. One-inch rulers.
3. Corrective underwear.
4. Half-car garages.
5. Saccharine substitute.
6. Three-piece suits for fish.
7. Fountain pens that give weather reports.

11
MAY I HAVE THE ENVELOPE, PLEASE?

CLINT EASTWOOD'S TWO FAVORITE FACIAL EXPRESSIONS

1. Angry.
2. Pissed.

6 THEME SHOWS MERV GRIFFIN HASN'T DONE YET

1. *A Salute to the PLO*
2. *Famous People with Pacemakers*
3. *In Search of Julius La Rosa*
4. *Rapping with Illiterates*
5. *A Tribute to Idaho* (with dancing potatoes)
6. *An Evening with the Pillsbury Doughboy*

3 PEOPLE YOU WOULDN'T WANT TO RUN INTO IN A DARK ALLEY

1. Lee Van Cleef.
2. Mr. Coffee.
3. Huckelberry Hound.

10 NAMES FOR HORROR MOVIES AIP HASN'T OPTIONED

1. *That Damn Wine Cellar*
2. *The Texax Chain Saw Something Scary*

3. *Still More Rats*
4. *It's Acne*
5. *The Beach That Had No Friends*
6. *Geeks! Geeks! Geeks!*
7. *Express-Line Rapist*
8. *The Oriental Driver*
9. *The Day the Cleaning Man Came*
10. *Some Call It Sleep*

3 WAYS TO TELL IF A NIGHTCLUB IS A FIRETRAP

1. There's an "I Brake for Drunks" bumper sticker plastered over the "Condemned" sign.
2. The torch singer wears an asbestos evening gown.
3. The chorus line is a pack of matched Dalmatians.

3 ONE-MAN SHOWS TO STAY AWAY FROM

1. *Billy Jean King Live*—a show built around the star's new line of "no-fault" cosmetics.
2. *Here They Are*—a glittering extravaganza starring Jacqueline Bisset, complete with fifty wet T-shirt changes.
3. *Rebel without a Movie*—an evening with Peter Fonda.

1 OUTFIT THAT LOOKS GOOD WITH A BOW TIE

1. A Garry Moore mask.

7 MAIN TOPICS OF CONVERSATION ON A SLOW *TONIGHT* SHOW

1. Orson Bean's head cold.

2. The lack of adequate street lighting in Bel Air.
3. Which has better delicatessens, Reno or Tahoe?
4. Rick Monday's real name.
5. Personal preferences in tux shirts.
6. Who's more macho, Gene Kelly or Gene Rayburn?
7. The financial status of Lola Falana's family.

8 ENTRIES FROM THE TULE, GREENLAND, FILM FESTIVAL

1. DER NACKTE BUNZ
   (The Naked Buns) Germany, 1977,
   103 minutes, color. In German with
   English subtitles.

    This film presents scenes from the life of an unhappily married baker (Jakov Bowie) who one day awakens to discover that his wife, vacationing in Belfast, has been blown to bits by the IRA. At first puzzled by the news—"Did she provoke them? Was her death an active choice?"—Jakov ends up running off with a delightfully scatterbrained blond cashier (Kirsten Burstyn).

    Director Jaime Moog loves enigmas and seems to follow the battle cry of the postwar German Very New Wave—"If you come to a dead end, exploit it!" As in his earlier films, *Let's Hear It for Bakers* and *Your Turn to Powder*; *My Turn to Glaze,* Moog is fascinated with the existential world of pastry—a microcosm peopled with idiots sufficiently out of the mainstream so as not to be tainted by it. Moog remains refreshingly untainted himself and has refined his appreciation for repetition and sloth into his most apathetic feature to date.

2. LA CASA del POLLO
   (Chicken House) Mexico, 1978,
   89 minutes, B&W. Silent.

    La Casa del Pollo is a serious statement about an irresponsible approach to life. Cinematographer Ramon Palom Lamon makes his directorial debut with this superbly staged-especially-for-the-cinema ballet production originally performed by the famed Ballet Folklorico.

The male corps de ballet is most effective in the hauntingly beautiful "Tostada" sequence and fiery "Avocado" mazurka, but the real standout performance comes from Anna-Maria Quintana, breathtakingly beautiful in the "Foxtrot to the Sun."

A visual masterpiece, *La Casa del Pollo* has run the critical gamut from "Lavishly lavish" (Rex Reed) to "What? No sound?" (John Simon).

3. THE BAD NEWS NEGROES
   U.S.A., 1978, 112 minutes. Color.

The United States Supreme Court recently ruled that "*The Bad News Negroes* violates no one's civil rights and appears to be an accurate representation, in documentary format, of what it must be like to live on the edge of a hellhole."

Based on an article appearing in the *National Enquirer*, *The Bad News Negroes* chronicles one day in the life of Mrs. Myrt Richey, an elderly widowed white woman living on the South Side of Chicago. Mrs. Richey wakes every morning to a daily ritual of motiveless malignity delivered in near-lethal doses by a band of roving Negroes. The Negroes, led by leader Lamont Beauville, are photographed parading directly in front of Mrs. Richey, actually sitting next to her on a park bench, and even brushing against her on a crowded subway car.

This movie is a fitting memorial to its maker, Robin Smith-Armstrong, who, while attending the premiere at the Watts Film Collective, was brutally murdered by a band of roving Negroes.

4. RIP ME KANGAROO
   APART, MATE
   Australia, 1976,
   19 minutes, color.

In Australian with English
accents.

Originally a hit tune, *Rip Me Kangaroo Apart, Mate* is
songwriter/director Gerry Powell's version of what happens
when eleven dingos (Australia's wild dogs) tear into a declawed
family pet.

5. LE FILS DE BOZO EST MORT!
   (Bozo's Kid Is Dead!)
   France, 1977, 592 minutes,
   B&W. In French with English
   subtitles.

Emil Bozo was the mayor of Ville d'Avis, France, from
1793-1881. Ville d'Avis, in the wine region of Bordeaux,
claims to have the highest median-age population of any city in
Europe, with the age of the average resident being 103. Ex-
panding on this premise, producer/director Jacques Rectifi
has fashioned a *cinéma-vérité* account of each citizen's reaction
to the death of Emil's son.

Rectifi says, "I would sneak up behind them with my
camera and tape recorder...and yell, '*Le fils de Bozo est mort!*' "
Their reactions (4,716), spontaneous, outrageous, pathetic
constitute the festival's longest, slowest-moving motion picture.

6. DON'T EAT YOURSELF FULL: THERE'S PIE BACK YET
   U.S.A., 88 minutes, color. In Pennsylvania
   Dutch with English subtitles.

It is 1945 and the war is over...or is it? Zionist hoodlum
David David-David is a desperate filmmaker who poses the
awful question, "If they sound like Germans, should they not
then die?"

Playing happy scene against sad, David-David toys with
our preconceptions and leads us down the garden path to what
appears to be an optimistic resolution. The machine-gun
murder of 417 happy picnickers reminds us that there are still
some surprises left in the American cinema.

7. LES FEMMES SANS TÊTES
   (The Headless Women) France, 1978,
   color. In French with English
   subtitles.

   Chuck Jourdan spent the better part of a year with the cast of the revue *80 Femmes 80*—backstage, on the Metro, at the gynecologist—shooting up over 18,000 miles of film.
   "The hardest part was the editing...to cut it down to eighty-nine minutes was...how do you say...uh...I don't know the word...a bitch!"
   There are still plenty of chicks in the final cut. Whether it's a cellulite treatment or checking for lumps, *Les Femmes sans Têtes* offers something for everybody.

8. HER MAJESTY'S STEERAGE
   Great Britain, 1978, 96 minutes;
   B&W.

   A rather fragmented account of documentarian Michael Woodburn's cramped confinement aboard Freddie Laker's no-frills Skytrain.

3 MIA FARROW MOVIES THAT WERE NEVER MADE

1. *The Jean Seberg Story.*
2. *St. Gidget.*
3. *Au Revoir Mon Career, Bonjour Mes Twins*

4 CELEBRITY ANSWERING-MACHINE MESSAGES

1. Colonel Harland Sanders: "Cluck, byuck, byuck, byuck... I'll get back to you..." Beep.
2. Mohammed Ali: "Float like a butterfly...sting like a bee...I can't talk now...I'm busy with me..." Beep.
3. Lina Wertmuller: "I'ma nota here...I'ma gonna go toa see

mya optometrista…anda pick up some more frame bleach…I calla you backa…" Beep.

4. Jerry Brown/Linda Ronstadt: "Hi…Jerry and I aren't home right now…he's out in Santa Monica being Grand Marshal of the Granola Days Parade…and I'm out looking for somebody who's not so busy…" Beep.

3 THIRD WORLD WOMEN MARLON BRANDO IS NOT ATTRACTED TO

1. Mongoloids.
2. Symbionese.
3. Nebraskans.

1 EPISODE OF *I LOVE LUCY* IN WHICH RICKY DIDN'T SING "CUBAN PETE"

1. Mr. Arnaz was out that day getting his green card renewed.

13 TELEVISION PILOTS THAT NEVER WENT TO SERIES

1. *Wok Concert.*
2. *The Bookies.*
3. *Gilligan's Peninsula.*
4. *Rich Man, Derelict.*
5. *One Sings, the Other Spits Up.*
6. *Complexion Detective.*
7. *David Berkowitz and Friends.*
8. *Kiss Me, I'm Comatose.*
9. *A Streetcar Named Bob Barker.*
10. *Let's Just Sit Here and Relax with You.*
11. *90 Minutes with Julius La Rosa.*
12. *The Hip Parade.*
13. *Top of the Mourning.*

Henry Winkler's 5 Favorite Greetings

1. "I am not the Fonz!"
2. "The Fonz I am not!"
3. "Not the Fonz am I!"
4. "I, the Fonz, am not!"
5. "Am the Fonz? Not I!"

3 People with Eyes at Half-Mast

1. Robert Mitchum.
2. Sylvester Stallone.
3. Tommy Lasorda.

4 Ways Howard Hughes Spent His Golden Years

1. Videotaping Jane Russell's bra commercials.
2. Sending a box of suckers to Melvin Dummar.
3. Deducting his live-in manicurist as a medical expense.
4. Getting Noah Dietrich confused with Marlene.

1 Actress Who Was Named after Days-of-the-Week Underwear and a Metal-Merging System

1. Tuesday Weld.

5 Theme Shows Tom Snyder Hasn't Done Yet

1. *Second Cousins to Lesbos.*
2. *Transsexual Translators.*

3. *Parents of Heterosexuals.*
4. *Hermaphroditic Gardeners.*
5. *Small-town Necrophiliacs.*

3 POPULAR ENTERTAINERS WHO SHOULDN'T HAVE FIRED THEIR INTERPRETERS

1. Desi Arnaz.
2. Andy Kaufman.
3. Ted Nugent.

9 CHEAP ACTOR'S QUOTES

1. "Genius does what it must do, talent does what it has to. Or is it the other way around?"
2. "There are two things I can always rely on in life: my ex-wife, and my craft."
3. "I think acting is a job, and my Mercedes is a car. I don't know, that's just how I feel."
4. "Ambisexuality isn't everything, it's the only thing."
5. "I don't have a brother, but if I had one, I'd want it to be Tony Orlando."
6. "Acting is like being on a train: some go coach, some go first class, and some go livestock."
7. "Well, there is Robert De Niro the man, and then there is Bobby De Niro, the ready-to-wear chain."
8. "Oh, I know Merv, but can you call it acting?"
9. "The only truly great actors in America are the actors who leave talk shows early, and then of course, the Negroes."

4 EXPOSÉS *SIXTY MINUTES* HASN'T DONE YET

1. Psychological dependence on Rosicrucian advertisements in magazines.

2. Premarital eating in Biafra.
3. Power struggles in the Hairdressers' Union.
4. The Formica boom—blessing or disaster?

5 WAYS THE WALTONS SIGN OFF IN ITALY

1. "Goodnight, Curly."
2. "Goodnight, Ju-Ju."
3. "Goodnight, Teets."
4. "Goodnight, 'The Babe.' "
5. "Goodnight, Fingers."

8 THINGS SCREENWRITERS DO WHEN THEY'RE NOT BUSY TAKING DRUGS

1. Use their best friend's credit cards for "research."
2. Pad the walls of their crash pad.
3. Check the obits for the competition.
4. Soak up local color at the Menninger Clinic.
5. Disguise themselves as Dorothy Parker when they go to the track.
6. Get extradited back to the Bronx on a morals charge.
7. Try to secure the rights to the Betty Hutton story.
8. Suck up to somebody who's been to Elaine's in New York.

3 PEOPLE WHO SAT THROUGH AN ENTIRE VISCONTI FILM

1. Luchino Visconti.
2. Antonia Visconti.
3. Helen Keller.

12
YOU CAN'T LIVE WITH 'EM...
YOU CAN'T LIVE WITHOUT 'EM

12 THINGS FOUND IN A BACHELOR'S APARTMENT

1. A terrarium full of change.
2. The complete works of Harold Robbins.
3. A 1,500-watt blow dryer.
4. Dust-covered Melmac dishes.
5. Air freshener.
6. A burgundy velour kimono robe (with hood.)
7. Dead house plants.
8. A lot of dry-cleaning bags.
9. Unpaid parking tickets.
10. Plenty of Oreos and milk.
11. A novelty cooking apron with "I'm the Boss!" printed on the front.
12. A copy of *So You Want to Date a Model*.

5 THINGS A GIRL MUST PACK ON HER HONEYMOON NIGHT

1. A push-up nude-colored bra. (Maybe he won't know the diff.)
2. Novocaine.
3. A scratch pad.
4. A thermos full of Pink Ladies.
5. Her ex-boyfriend's answering-service number.

9 WAYS IRISH GUYS LIKE TO JOCK IT UP ON THE WEEKEND

1. Throwing up on the doormat.

2. Giving the wife a half nelson.
3. Holding their breath to maintain their complexion.
4. Massaging their oldest son with a shillelagh.
5. Going skeet shooting with the wife's Waterford.
6. Giving body slams to the barmaid.
7. Jogging to confession.
8. Teaching their kids religion with holy flash cards.
9. Walking through metal detectors.

6 WAYS TO TELL IF YOUR GIRLFRIEND'S GOT LATIN BLOOD

1. She buys mascara by the pound.
2. She wears a push-up bra to bed.
3. Her idea of a foreign car is a Chevy.
4. She thinks wearing lace makes her look thinner.
5. She says prayers before putting on her garter belt.
6. She can only give the silent treatment for five minutes.

10 STORIES WOMEN MAKE UP AT THE RETURN DESK OF A DEPARTMENT STORE

1. "I would have brought it back earlier but I had a miscarriage."
2. "These hot rollers were a gift, but we don't use them at Synanon."
3. "I know it's all nylon, but when I bought them, I thought they had a cotton crotch."
4. "It may be monogrammed beautifully, but these aren't my initials."
5. "Of course there are makeup stains on it, that's how I bought it."
6. "If this was hand-painted, the rest of the body must have suffered a stroke."
7. "I like harem pants too, but Sinbad said they were the wrong color."

8. "I know everybody sweats, but this is an umbrella."
9. "No, I like it very much, but where I'm going, I won't need one."
10. "It didn't look good on Helen Reddy, and it won't look good on me."

5 Ways Guys Work Up a Sweat at the Y

1. Bullshitting about the scale.
2. Standing in front of the TV nude.
3. Slapping their belly and saying, "It's all muscle."
4. Putting on a jock to lie in the sun.
5. Cruising the weight room for a chair.

3 Things for a Woman Not to Do during Her Time of the Month

1. Have a slave sale with the kids.
2. Have a heart-to-heart with her mother-in-law.
3. Make a mental list of the kids who teased her in high school.

5 Reasons Why Women Resort to Babushkas

1. They like to pretend that they are Simone Signoret on location.
2. Someone once told them that they bore a striking resemblance to Valerie Harper.
3. They just got a job in a car wash.
4. Their hairdresser recommended it.
5. They couldn't bear to wake the rats.

3 Ways a Woman Can Undress Sexily Wearing Knee-High Stockings

1. Tell him it's a skin condition.
2. Kick them off can-can style.
3. Attach them to a frilly garter belt.

8 Things That Make a Woman Look Older

1. Cocktail rings.
2. Several babies.
3. Toilet-paper hair wraps.
4. A monocle.
5. Chest shimmies.
6. An expansive smallpox vaccination scar.
7. Floral-print nylon dresses complete with Sanka stains.
8. Sitting front row center at a Jim Nabors taping.

7 Ways Jewish Guys Jock It Up on the Weekend

1. Doing a full bench press with the wife's jewelry box.
2. Sitting in a sidewalk café sipping Perrier, bullshitting about shiksas.
3. Giving a Hebrew name to their colored maid.
4. Trying to decipher the pricing code in the new discount catalogue.
5. Armwrestling the mailman for postage due.
6. Trying to figure out why all physical laborers are gentiles.
7. Asking a hooker if she wants to dance the hora, and then laughing hysterically.

4 Things Not to Say to a Fellow Who Is Losing His Hair

1. "If that hairline recedes any more, your neck is going to look like it's blowing bubblegum!"
2. "If you're not careful, Brylcream is going to recall your head."
3. "I'd like to fix you up with Ethel Mertz."
4. "Excuse me, but is that a landing field for sparrows?"

3 Ways to Tell If a Middle-Aged Matron Was Once a Tart

1. If she gets teary-eyed and sentimental every time she gets into the back seat of an El Dorado.
2. If the only thing she wants for Christmas is a bottle of cologne and a twenty.
3. If she refers to her husband of thirty years as a john.

7 Things a Guy Must Pack on His Honeymoon Night

1. A six-pack of Detane.
2. A hot comb for fluffier chest curls.
3. A model-car kit.
4. New T-shirts.
5. His best friend.
6. A bottle of Stress Tabs.
7. A pair of crotchless ski pajamas.

6 Cute Little Ways Italian Men Say "I Love You"

1. Going out with the wife's sister.

2. Sending their in-laws a fish wrapped in newspapers.
3. Throwing their dinner against the wall and yelling, "Goat food!"
4. Spending the grocery money on pointed-toe shoes.
5. Burning her bathing suits.
6. Buying a new Easter outfit for himself.

7 PREREQUISITES FOR A JEWISH-AMERICAN PRINCESS

1. Memorizing the Torah while recovering from her rhinoplasty.
2. A life membership in the Eye Shadow of the Month Club.
3. Hanging out in medical-school cafeterias.
4. Getting her jeweler's loupe engraved with her initials.
5. Bronzing her old charge cards.
6. Taking a sunlamp along to her therapy sessions.
7. Flying to the Bahamas to recover from a bad period.

13
YE LITTLE ONES

3 REASONS NOT TO HAVE CHILDREN

1. They're hard on shoes.
2. They look like midgets.
3. The urine level in your swimming pool increases markedly.

6 PREREQUISITES FOR A SUMMER-CAMP COUNSELOR

1. Ability not to act self-conscious in a loincloth.
2. Capacity to explain about the birds and the bees using Indian sign language.
3. Penchant for cut-off sweatshirts.
4. Willingness to permit a particularly spiteful child to go without his life jacket.
5. Sincere belief that crewcuts do make you cooler.
6. Copy of *One Hundred and One Uses for Braided Vinyl Key Chains*.

4 WAYS TO TELL IF YOUR SON IS
FLUNKING OUT OF COLLEGE

1. His last report card was postmarked "Attica."
2. You see his picture on an Army recruiting poster.
3. He thinks carrying a full load is a bad case of constipation.
4. The last paperback he read was "TV Guide."

6 NAMES FOR CHILDREN OF THE LATE '60s

1. Moon Unit.

2. Granola.
3. Macra May.
4. Strobe.
5. Ellis Dee.
6. Monongahela.

4 THINGS BOY SCOUTS SHOULD WATCH OUT FOR

1. Their pack leader.
2. Having to dress up like an Injun.
3. The centerfold in *National Geographic*.
4. Straddle latrines.

4 THINGS GIRL SCOUTS SHOULD WATCH OUT FOR

1. The fluctuating cookie market.
2. Hot merit badges.
3. The LAPD.
4. Brownies.

3 ALTERNATIVES TO DAY-CARE CENTERS

1. The broom closet.
2. Grandma.
3. The back burner.

3 ENTERTAINERS WHO WEREN'T BLACKLISTED IN THE '50s

1. Kukla.
2. Fran.
3. Ollie.

3 EXCUSES TO GIVE TO GET OUT OF GYM CLASS

1. Your mom is having a baby and you have got to go home and watch.
2. A burglar broke into your home and stole your gym clothes.
3. The owner of the malt shop died and you were asked to be a pallbearer.

5 WAYS TO TELL IF A CHILD IS ABUSED

1. The kid is paying his parents protection money.
2. He's on a first-name basis with the staff of the emergency room.
3. His Timex has stopped ticking.
4. When his friends ask, "What are you doing?" he replies, "Ten to life."
5. His idea of a vacation is room service in the broom closet.

3 THINGS JOHN BOY NEVER SAID TO HIS PARENTS

1. "You and whose Army?"
2. "Goodnight, Spaz."
3. "Kiss my mole!"

7 REMARKS TEACHERS LOVE TO WRITE ON TEST PAPERS

1. "See me!"
2. "Very good...*if original*."
3. "I'm sure you'll be very happy in the Army."
4. "I don't read chicken scratch."
5. "Someone's been watching too much television!"
6. "Do you really think Willy Bobo is suitable material for an essay?"
7. "F+...Now let's see your father bail you out of this one!"

4 THINGS TO KEEP ON HAND FOR THE BABYSITTER

1. T-shirts with the kids' names on them.
2. Plenty of soft drinks with straws.
3. A pay phone.
4. A guest book.

5 WAYS TO KEEP YOUR DAUGHTER FROM MARRYING AN ETHNIC MINORITY

1. Keep referring to her boyfriend as "the little Injun that could."
2. Tell her you don't want your grandchildren to look like zebras.
3. Scare some sense into her by saying, "If you marry him, you'll want to get married again an hour later."
4. Tell her the only cultural advantage is a lifetime bullfight pass.
5. Tell her the sex may be good, but the barbecue sauce stains.

5 TOYS YOUR PARENTS WOULDN'T BUY FOR YOU WHEN YOU WERE A KID

1. Blasting caps.
2. A Stradivarius.
3. A machete.
4. A dude ranch.
5. Annette Funicello.

10 THINGS AIR FORCE BRATS DO IN THEIR SPARE TIME

1. Split for the coast.
2. Clean out their locker.
3. Order new stationery.
4. Withdraw the funds from their Christmas Club.
5. Reread the Joan Fontaine autobiography, *No Bed of Roses*.

6. Rearrange the pins on the map.
7. Oil the wheels on the buffet.
8. Try to get a handle on their accent.
9. Call Mom "Jezebel."
10. Search for a one-armed man.

6 Things Your Kids Do That Make You Wonder If There Was a Mix-up at the Maternity Hospital

1. Shave the kitten and dress him up like a Hare Krishna.
2. Take the brakes off Grandma's wheelchair.
3. Do their Patty McCormack impression from *The Bad Seed*.
4. Dig a mantrap for the Japanese gardener.
5. Knock up your sister-in-law.
6. Sell urine for two cents a glass at their lemonade stand.

5 True Lies Your Mother Told You

1. "All boys have Russian hands and Roman fingers."
2. "When you grow up and get married, your husband will want one thing and you won't like it."
3. "I think there was a mix-up at the hospital."
4. "Don't ever wear patent-leather shoes; the boys will look up your skirt."
5. "Grandpa isn't dead; he's just sleeping."

3 Entries from 14-Year-Old Debbie Mullens's Diary

1. Dear Diary,
   Today is probably the most awful day of my life. My current best friend, Joanie P., started going steady with Steve D. She knew I liked Steve a real lot. It was a real gross thing to do to me, so I will never speak to her again, except maybe in

gym class, because we're both in charge of the locker room this week. Yccch, what a creep she turned out to be. At least I still have Parker Stevenson. I guess that should be enough for any girl. I figured out today that the P.S. you put on letters, well, now when I write that, it will stand for Parker Stevenson. Pretty good, huh?

I went to the shopping center today with Linda, and I stole some lip gloss, and a bathing suit. The bathing suit was too big for me, so I'm going to put it away and give it to my mom for Mother's Day. She would have a cow if she knew where it came from. My birthday's coming in four more days and my mom and dad said they would take me and a friend to Disneyland. I was going to take Joanie, but now I would die first.

Debbie

P.S.   I love him.

2. Dear Diary,

I went to the beach today, and I got a sunburn. On the way home on the bus, my bottle of baby oil and iodine broke and got all over my cover-up right in a certain place. It looked like I had the curse, and I was so embarrassed, I almost died.

I had a dream last night about Parker Stevenson, and in the dream we went to the shopping center together and he stole a friendship ring and gave it to me. It was the best dream I ever had. I drove to the store with my mom this afternoon and we were at a stoplight and Billy R., who is only the cutest guy in the whole entire junior high school, was riding by on his skateboard. I didn't want him to see me in the same car with my mom so I hid down on the floor. I don't think he saw me, but my mom got really crazy and told me I was acting immature. I think it would have been more immature if he had seen me with my mom, but I didn't try and explain that to her, because lately I try not to talk to her much, unless no one is watching.

Love, Debbie

P.S.   Parker is the cutest guy in the world, but I also like Ron Cey a lot too. I guess if Parker Stevenson ever died that Ron Cey would be the cutest guy in the world.

77

3. Dear Diary,

It's pretty late and I still have some homework to do, but the greatest thing happened today and I am so happy I made my face break out; it always does when I get excited. That's why I didn't make the cheerleading squad, I got so nervous at tryouts that my face broke out right there in front of the principal and everybody. Anyway, like my brother Jackie always says, "They can put Debbie in jail, but they can't stop her face from breaking out." Ycccch.

Back to today. I was at the mall with Joanie P. and Rhonda H. and some other girls from school when a policewoman grabbed Rhonda by the arm and caught her shoplifting. I was so scared I thought I'd throw up. Lucky for Rhonda she didn't steal anything yet and the lady had to let her go. Rhonda was crying and everything so afterward Joanie and me took her to McDonald's and bought her a banana shake. It was perfect because Rhonda was really going bananas. Ha. Ha.

Now the good part. While we were drinking our shakes this real cute guy driving a ten-speed bike came up to our table and sat down with us. His name is Dean and he has a pet ocelot at home. Anyway, he asked me to go to the movies on Saturday. He looks just like David Soul's son. I can't wait until Saturday. I wish I had something to wear. Maybe I'll go to the mall tomorrow and get something on five-finger discount.

Love ya,
Debbie

14
80 YEARS YOUNG

10 Behavioral Tips for Attending a Nursing-Home Dance

1. Don't let it bother you when someone dribbles on your organza housecoat.
2. Don't try to look too much like Rosemary DeCamp.
3. Don't ask, "Are you a widower?"
4. Don't be afraid to lead.
5. Brush up on your CPR techniques.
6. Don't let anyone take your pulse.
7. Don't wear a support bra. (Remember, you want your man to like you for you.)
8. Avoid the guys that are hanging around the oxygen tank.
9. Remember to blot your face powder.
10. When he says he's a vet, don't ask what war.

5 Things a Sexagenarian Widower Does in His Spare Time

1. Moves to Vegas.
2. Signs up for square dancing at the senior citizens' hall.
3. Thinks up radical solutions to the racial problem.
4. Blows his entire Social Security check on sympathy cards.
5. Loses his funeral plot in a pinochle game.

5 Gifts for a Mobile-Home Warming

1. A plastic flamingo.
2. A staircase.

3. A ceramic cat.
4. A three-pack of beer.
5. A first edition of the *Meals on Wheels* cookbook.

7 THINGS BLUE-HAIRED LADIES TALK ABOUT AT MATINEES

1. Their Ayds habit.
2. Their grandson's graduation suit.
3. The new window at Lane Bryant.
4. How to "one-hand" an Ace bandage.
5. The striking resemblance between Engelbert Humperdinck and John Gilbert.
6. Their new matching pillbox hat and collapsible cup.
7. Their collection of hospital ID bracelets.

3 WEALTHY FELINES WHO DIED AND LEFT THEIR FORTUNES TO PEOPLE

1. HUNTER THE CAT (1968-1971)   CALICO
   UNITED STATES

   Hunter was a shrewd investor with plenty of business savvy and got in on the ground floor of an aerosol-can company. He amassed an estimated estate of $2,500,000 in record time. Unfortunately, at the peak of his success he suffered an untimely death. Although the cat had no living blood relatives, he willed his entire estate to his roommate and constant companion, Mrs. Ella Weaver of Hawthorne, California.

   Mrs. Weaver was apparently so shaken by the sad tidings that she simply converted most of the inheritance into nickels, packed the money into suitcases, and hopped an airplane to Las Vegas.

2. ALTHEA THE CAT   (1951-1978)   PERSIAN
   ENGLAND
   Whilst Althea was on her death basket, she put her paw

print on a new will, which superseded the document drawn up by her barrister and chief adviser, Lord P.R. Bridges. The new will named Mrs. Sylvester Byrd as chief beneficiary. Althea's estate was quite a tidy sum. Lord Bridges and other close chums were highly indignant when they heard of this strange turn of events. Althea and Mrs. Byrd had always been rival hostesses in the county. Some of the surrounding circumstances of the feline's death seemed quite odd.

An inquest was held, but alas, the judge dismissed the case on lack of evidence. Some mystery still shrouds the demise of the charming and erudite Althea the Cat.

3. GRUMPI THE CAT   ITALO-CALICO   (1975-1975)
UNITED STATES

When Grumpi met his maker and left his six-figure fortune to Mrs. Kitty Klatch of Chicago, Illinois, Mrs. Klatch went totally berserk. She went into a coma, had to be hospitalized, and didn't regain consciousness for forty-eight hours. Reporters stood by in hospital corridors waiting to interview the heiress. When Mrs. Klatch came to, she stated flatly, "No comment," and asked the nurse to fetch her a pair of very dark sunglasses. It is rumored that Grumpi had syndicate connections.

14 EVENTS AT THE 1980 SPECIAL SENIOR CITIZENS' OLYMPICS

1. Pitching gallstones.
2. Running to the toilet.
3. The teeth put.
4. Cane vaulting.
5. Wrestling a walker.
6. The fifty-yard shake.
7. Coupon clipping.
8. Remembering grandchildren's names.
9. Channel switching.
10. Long-distance telephone dialing.

11. Age guessing.
12. Insulting the nurses.
13. The trans living room walking race.
14. The best back wins events.

1 THING A MEXICAN MAN OVER SIXTY-FIVE IS CALLED

1. A señor citizen.

3 THINGS THAT MAKE IT DIFFICULT TO GIVE MOUTH-TO-MOUTH RESUSCITATION

1. The onion dip.
2. The victim is rather plain and unattractive.
3. You don't know where it's been.

5 THINGS TO LOOK FOR IN A FUNERAL PLOT

1. Convenient bus lines.
2. Twenty-four-hour florist on the premises.
3. Location in a "good neighborhood."
4. Leg room.
5. No country music.

5 ALTERNATIVE CAREERS FOR GEORGE JESSEL

1. Critiquing the staff at the Old Motion Picture Home.
2. Master of ceremonies at the annual Miss Vapido contest.
3. Assistant manager of the Hollywood Wax Museum.
4. Head usher at Radio City Music Hall.
5. Art director for *Photoplay*.

11 REQUIREMENTS FOR THRIFT-SHOP EMPLOYEES

1. Blue/gray hair.
2. Their own collection of pastel smocks.
3. The ability to one-hand a safety pin.
4. A hearing defect.
5. Adequate ventilation in their orthopedic shoes.
6. Matching, oversized, coral-colored, plastic necklace and earrings.
7. A large spray bottle of Heaven Sent.
8. A distinctive walk.
9. Membership in Emmett Kelly's Lips of the World Club.
10. Fingernails with Gothic edges for seam ripping.
11. A coffee mug with "Grandma Power" written on the side.

15
I COULD HAVE BEEN
A CONTENDER

3 OCCUPATIONS POPULAR WITH EX-PRIZEFIGHTERS

1. Greeter in Vegas.
2. Greeter in Reno.
3. Greeter in Atlantic City.

3 CELEBRITIES WHO STUDIED ACTING WITH ELIOT JANEWAY

1. Bruce Jenner.
2. O. J. Simpson.
3. Jerry Ford.

8 LINES OF CONVERSATION OVERHEARD WHILE WAITING IN LINE FOR HOCKEY TICKETS

1. "If you think this turtleneck is neat, you should see the one I've got on underneath it."
2. "Correct me if I'm wrong, but isn't Bobby Orr a Scientologist?"
3. "Five dollars says your wife does *not* know where you are tonight."
4. "Yeah?...I'd like to high-stick *her!*"
5. "It's getting awfully chilly."
6. "Which one of the Howe twins is older?"
7. "Butch Goring does look like Ryan O'Neal!"
8. "No, no, no...Al Melgaard is the *organist!*"

4 Things Guys Look for in a Bookie

1. He speaks English without a trace of a Chicago accent.
2. He can keep his lip buttoned.
3. He keeps his accounts on flash paper.
4. He doesn't wear dark glasses inside.

3 People Not to Take on a Ride through the Tunnel of Love

1. Richard Speck.
2. Boo Radley.
3. Steve Garvey.

3 Ways to Spot a Former Dust Bowl Refugee

1. He is a close personal friend of Dennis Weaver's.
2. He gets maudlin every time he sees a flatbed truck.
3. He's still looking for Rose of Sharon.

6 Things Security Guards Do with Their Spare Time

1. Analyze handwriting.
2. Grouse about losing their fingers.
3. Punch extra holes in their belt.
4. Stare in the mirror saying, "You talkin' to me?"
5. Inspect their chins for speed bumps.
6. Paint coffee stains on their wind-up teeth.

16
TAKE ME TO YOUR LEADER

4 FIRST-PERSON ACCOUNTS OF A UFO SIGHTING IN TOPEKA, KANSAS

1. Me and my beau Errol were porch-sitting that night. Errol kissed me and I started to feel a very strange heat. And I remember thinkin', "Hot dog, I love Errol." Then a red glow came over us, both Errol and me. I thought it was time to stop, but it weren't. Then this big flyin' thing that looked like a big piece of hard candy came by. This is definitely the biggest thing that's happened in these parts since Leon's bib overalls caught fire last spring.

    Jeffina Dunne

2. My wife was outdoors hanging the clothes and I was in the kitchen cleaning catfish. All of a sudden Mama hollers, "Come running, there's a UFO out here!" I thought...wait one dad-burned minute, that can't be, and of course Mama's been pestering me for her own specialty dress shop. I yelled back, "The hell you say...I'll bet you one specialty dress shop that you been taking them pain pills Doc Swanson gave you, Verna." That's my wife's name, Verna, even though I call her Mama most times. So not only did I see this most amazing thing, but we are now the proud owners of a specialty dress shop, sizes sixteen to twenty-two and half sizes.

    Edgar Sheffler

3. My brother drowned the week before and I was just getting over the heebie-jeebies on that one when my half-son, Don L., came whopping and waving about like a banshee up the dirt path. He yelled, "Hey, half-dad, half-dad...come take a gander at this." I looked yonder and right above Brewer's Gulch I saw what seemed to be a giant cold-cream jar with big picture

windows floating across the sky, and I don't drink neither. I got enough trouble trying to raise two half-kids.

Wayne Kimball

4. Now I saw something about two and a half days ago. Now I ain't saying it was and I ain't saying it wasn't. But I tell you something. I shouldn't be seeing nothing out of the ordinary with the kind of property taxes I'm paying around here.

Hopkin Ashmore

4 Ways to Spot a Phony Psychic

1. She asks you to call her your sidekick.
2. She's incorporated.
3. She speaks perfect English and wears her skirts above the knee.
4. She has never seen the musical *Gypsy*.

6 Sympathetic Things to Say to Air-Heads

1. "That's okay, dear, your first name is the important one."
2. "What are you going to do for the talent segment of the contest?"
3. "Manicuring *is* an honorable profession!"
4. "I don't think taking up pipesmoking will help."
5. "You must be Mrs. Sugardaddy."
6. "I agree, game shows are informative."

6 Favorite Overlooked Sights

1. The look on your dad's face when he heard you were convicted of murder one.
2. The look on your pimp's face when you tell him to run a tab.

3. The look on your insurance agent's face when you tell him he has bad skin.
4. The look on your husband's face when you tell him *he* gets the kids.
5. The look on Jimmy Carter's face when he learns his escort planes are Russian MiGs.
6. The look on Bob Dylan's face when he saw the review for *Reynaldo and Clara*.

3 Last Resorts after You've Tried EST, TM, Scientology, and Esalen

1. Wringing your hands.
2. A good book.
3. *Sesame Street*.

3 Things Chubs Do When They're Alone in a Public Restroom

1. They grease down the sides of the stall for easy entry.
2. They check out the mirror for new love handles.
3. They check their beehive hairdo for an emergency candy stash.

10 Things S.F. Freaks Do in Their Spare Time

1. Hold court at the all-night newsstand.
2. Stop by the optometrist to get their eyes dilated.
3. Live alone.
4. Be on call for the local police lineup.
5. Try to guess Michael Rennie's weight in *The Day the Earth Stood Still*.
6. Hang out at the schoolyard and stalk big-eared girls.

7. Polish their "Gene Roddenberry is a Friend of Mine" belt buckles.
8. Check in with the family physician for an "enthusiasm bypass."
9. Spot check their salads for extra-large pea pods.
10. Blow their unemployment checks on Mars Bars.

17
POLITICIANS AND BEAUTICIANS

9 OF JERRY BROWN'S FAVORITE ZEN SAYINGS

1. "Boy, are my dogs tired!"
2. "Boy, do I feel peaceful."
3. "Boy, can Linda sing swell, huh."
4. "Boy, is Malibu hot this time of year."
5. "Boy, is this guacamole good."
6. "Boy, is Jeff Wald short."
7. "Boy, am I an alternative governor."
8. "Boy, am I busy."
9. "Boy, am I young to be president."

3 PHRASES MOST OFTEN HEARD IN A BEAUTY SALON

1. "You're burning my hair."
2. "If I have to walk out of here like this, I'll just die!"
3. "But I didn't want a Mohawk."

3 MEXICAN-AMERICANS WHO DO NOT OWN VELVET JFK RUGS

1. Chico Rodriguez, Fresno, Calif. Chico had one but sold it to buy tripe and fender skirts for his Chevy.
2. Arturo Chavez, Chicago, Ill. Arturo owns an RFK rug; his JFK is on permanent loan to the Guggenheim Museum.
3. Pancho "You Talkin' to Me" Casado, Beverly Hills, Calif. Hates California; it's cold and it's damp.

3 OF IDI AMIN'S FAVORITE HOBBIES

1. Mainlining penicillin.
2. Interrogating enemies on a Hibachi.
3. Playing a Jew's harp while watching *Holocaust*.

3 WAYS TO TELL IF A POLITICAL CARTOONIST HAS GONE STALE

1. The Russian Bear has Khrushchev's face.
2. Every character he draws talks to God.
3. He's still rendering H. R. Haldeman with a crewcut.

3 OF BELLA ABZUG'S FAVORITE SUBSTITUTES FOR HATS

1. A hubcap.
2. Oven mittens (one at a time).
3. A medium-size Queen Anne chair.

1 MACROBIOTIC NAME FOR A GOVERNOR'S SISTER

1. Kathleen Brown Rice.

4 TESTIMONIALS FOR ARBUCKLE WEIGHT-LOSS PRODUCTS

1.   "Just last week I tipped the scales at 250 lbs....Today I weigh 158 lbs. I can now go to an Al Martino concert without buying two tickets, thanks to Arbuckle pills."

Russel Busby
(47 years old)

2.　　"I was so fat my husband called me his Little Divan. Now he calls me his Little Divine. Thanks to Arbuckle I lost more pounds than I can count!"

Mary Dee Williams
(35 years old)

3.　　"I used to be so fat that my husband, a very famous entertainer with a name too famous to print, although he does play Vegas twice a year, called me an embarrassing Oink-Oink and said I was ruining his career. Well, that was last year, and now my husband is on the skids and we are divorced. Thanks to Arbuckle I am down to a svelt 97 lbs., and am about to be married again real soon."

Dianna M.
(age unknown)

4.　　"My family talked me into using Arbuckle and I haven't lost a pound, but, boy, am I wired for sound."

Minnie Tailor
(66 years young)

7 SUPERSTITIONS POPULAR AMONG POLICE CHIEFS

1. A purple Cadillac crossing your path means your house will be broken into.
2. Whistling in your pajamas means you're not sleepy.
3. Sitting through a Wayne Newton show for the third time causes listlessness.
4. Opening an umbrella in your pants is bad luck.
5. If you get a check in the mail, it means you're coming into money.
6. If you file for divorce, it means there's trouble at home.
7. If you have a dream about Jack Ruby, it means a close relative will die and leave you their jewelry.

5 Things Not to Say to the Wife When She Comes Home from the Beauty Salon

1. "Oh, too bad, they couldn't take you."
2. "I don't care if you did see a flat top and fenders in *Vogue!*"
3. "David Bowie can get away with it, you can't."
4. "Okay, you've had your fun, now take that fright wig back where you got it."
5. "I hope you have plenty of scarves."

18
NONE DARE CALL IT NEWS

9 HEADLINES THE *NATIONAL ENQUIRER* TOOK A PASS ON

1. Informed Sources Reveal Ike Was a Negro.
2. Dead Chihuahua Found in Charo's Hair.
3. Bishop Sheen Arrested in Disco Scandal.
4. Bernadette Devlin Claims No Knowledge of IRS Activities.
5. Bess Myerson to Change Hairdo.
6. Scientists Announce, "Eating Pasta May Cause Wife Abuse."
7. Latest College Fad: Swallowing Goldbergs.
8. Brain Damage Linked to Wearing of Signature Scarves.
9. Oriental Americans Held in Detention Camps on Traffic Charges.

4 CLASSIFIED APARTMENT ADS TO STAY AWAY FROM

1. One bedroom. Everything a nursing home has except the rope burns. Senior citizens welcome. Quiet building in industrial neighborhood.
2. Large single. Phone plugs already ripped out. Barred window, perfect for shut-ins. $150 per.
3. Rustic fixer-upper. 8 bdrms. $30 per month. Call Grace after four a.m.
4. Wanted: Roommate to share great apartment. Your share $300. My share $150. Air Force brat.

5 WAYS GRETA GARBO SPENDS HER SATURDAY MORNINGS

1. Cruising Saks' for a new pair of shades.

2. Getting her trench coat relined.
3. Calling Tom Tryon and giving him what for.
4. Reading *What Ever Happened to…* books.
5. Going to a psychic to get in touch with Joan Crawford.

3 EXCERPTS FROM HENNA RENZ'S GOSSIP COLUMN

DATELINE HOLLYWOOD ....
by Henna Renz

1.   Well, what little starlet with the initials M.D., whose dress size is five (so she says), whose ex-husband is President of Monarch Pictures, whose astrological sign is Taurus (and she is full of bull), whose address is 1506 N. Sweetzer, West Hollywood (not even Beverly Hills, poor dear)…is seeing a new facial expert whose techniques are out of this world, if you read me.

This little girl is in for a rude awakening. This time she is really playing with fire. So, from Henna to you, darling, just a little word to the wise. I would stop worrying about that pretty little face of yours, and concentrate on your two other assets, if you follow my lead.

And speaking of assets, while we're on the subject, a certain superstar writer, actor, director, producer, maitre d' (this guy is a real cingo threat) spent a weekend on the county a few days ago. He was arrested for being just too, too talented. Ha, ha, darlings, your Henna's just joking. This super threat to the motion-picture industry was picked up on a morals charge. It seems he doesn't have any.

And to you, sir, all I can say is, you should be ashamed of yourself. We know you geniuses have your problems, and God forbid, if it weren't for people like you, where would Lotus Land be? But two German shepherds, a twelve-year-old boy, and a female member of the Symbionese Liberation Army (former) is all too, too much for any of us to understand. Didn't you read *Hollywood Babylon*, sir? Does the name Fatty Arbuckle mean anything to you? Does the name Cubby mean anything to you? Ramon Novarro? Huh? Huh? Huh? Do you want to be remembered not for your contributions to the movie biz, but for your obsession with women's lingerie, or a quick go-around with a bow-wow? Well, enough on that, and I hope I've helped.

On an upbeat note, and I can tell you readers that last paragraph took a lot out of me, I have some really delightful news to report. Joan Fontaine and sis Olivia deHavilland have just had a long heart-to-heart and are burying the hatchet. The two sisters have been bickering for years because it seems that Olivia was olive-complected and Joan wasn't. Joan was really peeved over that one, but Olivia recently made the first move, and sent Joan a beautiful silk jacket with a charming embroidered volcano on the back, and the words "EO's Sushi Bar" printed on it. It seems to have done the trick. My congrats to both of you gals for being so damned sensible.

Congrats to Power Pictures artist Roberto Massetti for changing his name back to Hoby Gillman. Good move, Roberto, or should I say Hoby. We knew that trend in Italian actors wouldn't last forever. They are foreigners, for Christ's sakes, and who needs them? Good luck to you, kid.

And Henna's bit of wisdom for today is: Adolphe Menjou isn't alive anymore, I think. Adolphe, if you're out there, and I'm wrong, give me a jingle. I'd love to hear your voice again.

Now for the answer to yesterday's film quiz: Dino, Desi, and Billy.

DATELINE HOLLYWOOD ....
By Henna Renz

2.   We open our column today on a sad note, friends. All our prayers and best regards go to Shaun Cassidy today, who is convalescing at St. Johns of Publicity Hospital here in the heart of Hollywoodland.

Poor Shaun has an advanced case of satin rash. But the doctors say to keep those fingers crossed.

The family is holding a bedside vigil. Everyone, including Shaun's big brother David (you remember him), is there.

David is a big source of consolation to Shaun because he had quiana rash years ago and had to be hospitalized as well.

There is some speculation that these cloth infections could be hereditary in the Cassidy family.

In lieu of flowers, say a silent prayer that Shirley Jones' marriage to Marty Engels takes.

Shaun's grandad, Hopalong, was so concerned he had to ride the range a couple of times before he could calm down.

And on a happier note, say *bon voyage* to veteran character actor Willie Willie, who went to his final rest this last Tuesday. Willie shot to stardom on that old *I'm Dickens, He's Hugo* Show. Willie, of course, played Victor Hugo and did some bang-up job. I might add Willie's widow Lily was grief-stricken to beat the band. She is quoted as saying, "With Willie gone, there will be more left for me." I get a lump in my throat and my pocketbook when I think about that grand old girl. Hats off to you, Lily.

In lieu of flowers, send donations to the R.J. Reynolds Company, Salem, North Carolina. He is survived by wife, Lily, and his longtime ward, Bubbles Latour.

And on an upbeat note, in tinseltown today, Elvis Costello and Bud Abbott are joining forces again. Praise be!!! You boys have been apart too long. Maybe Robert Q. Lewis and Dean Martin will take the lead from you and get back on the right track. My best to all four of you, and, of course, your loved ones, too.

Answer to my filmland quiz from yesterday: Barbara Stanwyck and Mick Fleetwood.

By the way, just yesterday in my column I printed a story about Joan Fontaine and her big sis Olivia deHavilland putting an end to their longtime quarreling. I hate to admit it, readers, but the girls are still at it, according to reliable sources. The story about the silk oriental jacket was all true except the names. It seems the two bickersons in that case were Joni Mitchell and her gardener.

DATELINE CAMARILLO STATE MENTAL HOSPITAL ....
By Henna Renz

3.   Confidential to you: What well-known Hollywood gossip columnist has finally gone off the deep end? It's a pity that certain film folks don't realize that a certain Hollywood col-

umnist has her own cross to bear. You think dying your hair platinum blond and retouching the roots every four to six weeks is easy? You think wearing strapless, sequined evening gowns when you are a full-figured girl is easy? I know no one promised her a rose garden, but God knows that there is only so much one woman can take. All this lady is looking for is a little understanding. I'm talking to you out there. You heard me!!

Some people are worse offenders than others. I don't want to name names, but...For instance, you, Dinah, Merv, and Mike. You, Dinah, don't you remember when I came on your show and you asked every panelist on the show, including Mel Tillis, to sing a duet with you, but did you ever ask me? No, never!

And you, Mike, you asked Willie Willie (even though you knew he was my first husband) to co-host your show with you, but did you ever think of asking me? No, never!!!

And, Merv, where was I when you did that tribute to Libras? Where was I? I'll tell you where I was. I was home crying my eyes out. And I'll tell you something else. What!!! Clam dip!!! I don't even like clam dip.

And another thing, you know what I was thinking of the other day? When I was a little girl my mother would dress me in pink organza, always pink because she said it went well with my eyes, and white cotton gloves, all starched and nice, and little shiny Mary Jane pumps with straps. And all day long I would sit, like a little princess, just sit and sit and sit....I told you to get that goddam clam dip out of here!!!

Pussy cat in the tree
Don't fall down on your knee
Dip dip dip
Brum brum brum
Come on, Hoss, let's get back to the Ponderosa....

3 MIMEOGRAPHED WASP CHRISTMAS LETTERS

1. Brooke and Carter Carter's:
   December 13, 1978

To our Friends...

Well, well, well, it's that time of year again. Santa's hitching up the reindeer and all that.

Just to bring you up to date on the past year's events:

1978 started off with a bang when Carter, Jr., drove his brand-new Porsche off Valley View Drive. He was a little peeved at us because we wouldn't allow him to take flying lessons. Boys will be boys, you know. It took two doubles to calm Carter, Sr., down.

Last spring our little princess, Diana, was elected Queen of the May, which was a great honor. Already she's boasting "loads of contacts," whatever that means.

In October the Community Theater here put on their annual play and they asked Carter, Sr., to play the lead. Can you feature that? My Carter a star? The production they chose was *Lost Weekend*, and Carter played the Ray Milland part. When he heard the news, he was so thrilled that it took three doubles to calm him down.

I have some very special news I would like to share with all of you. I had always wanted to try psychoanalysis, and I finally got the courage to go into therapy this year. My very special news is that I have been having an affair with Carter, Sr.'s, boss for fourteen years and with the help of my analyst I've finally been able to break it off. When I told Carter, he was so excited it took four doubles to calm him down.

We really have a lot to be thankful for as we enter this holiday season. We all have our health except for poor Carter, Sr. He would love to hear from you. Please write to him in care of the Detoxification Center in Champagne, Illinois. He'll be so excited, I don't know what it will take to calm him down.

Love and candy canes,
The Carters

2. Ward and June Cleaver's:
December 2, 1978
Seasons Greetings!

Christmas is just around the corner and the snow's on the ground and all that.

What a year it's been!

Ward is now a veep at Cleaver, Carter, and Bancroft law firm. We are sure by now you've heard the news about poor Carter Carter. The big question is, who will host this year's Tom & Jerry party?

This last summer, we had a real treat. Inspired by seeing that colored show, *Roots*, we flew off to England to get our genealogy traced. What an experience!!! I would have enjoyed it more if it wasn't for the language barrier. Anyway...it turns out the Cleavers are from noble blood and Ward may even have a title. (I've had a title for him for years, if you get my drift.)

We are a little lonely this Christmas because, as I'm sure all of you remember, we've never had any children to enjoy the holidays with. Ward really takes our childlessness to heart. Most afternoons he just mopes around the neighborhood schoolyard looking for the little moppet we never had, or I should say, he's never had.

I've got to run. The paperboy is here standing before me, a mass of masculine, sinewy flesh...his hair askew...his skin-tight Levi's pulling against the huge bulge in his pants and emphasizing that pulsing throb even more...I promised the little dickens I'd teach him the metric system.

Yours in Christmas,
Ward & June Cleaver

3. Betty and Bob Thomas':
    December 15, 1978
    Dear Ones,
      Our holidays are very sad this year because Pepi won't be with us. We hope there are plenty of doggie treats in heaven.

Blue about Christmas,
The Thomases

12 SIGNS OF THE UNDISCOVERED ZODIAC AND THEIR FORECAST FOR THE MONTH OF JUNE — ANY YEAR

ZEBRA
1. The Stripe. January

Hot, hot, hot. This month is going to be a scorcher. All fair-skinned Zebras (and all Zebras are fair-skinned) better stock up on your sunscreen lotion, and/or stay indoors.

You hear you are going to get some reward for a criminal you have turned in. Don't spend it all in one place; you know Zebras aren't exactly known for their good sense in financial affairs.

Since you were born under the Stripe, make sure you check with your eye doctor this month.

If you are planning to travel in June, try to confine it to the Andes and/or Bavaria.

New romance coming your way about two a.m. on the morning of the 18th.

Advice to you Stripes: Stay away from all Blotto the Drunks this month; the stars forecast a bender for them.

PENGUIN
2. The Tux. February

Brrrr...June is going to be a chilly month for all you Tuxes. Last month you faced many problems, including the inevitable conflict with Panda the Cosmetologist. Not to worry, Pandas are very superficial. One of them will be with you until mid-June. Near the 20th you will make a decision which will ensure world peace.

Those of you Penguins on the cusp of Eggplant will be noshing on an abundance of cold cuts and frozen TV dinners this month. There will be plenty of black-tie events in June, which should make you very happy.

Estrangement is the key.

Your lucky days are Columbus and Arbor.

BLOTTO
3. The Drunk. March

Restlessness could cause you to fall from a twenty story building, in June. You could be dissatisfied with your fall. You long for a holiday but lack the right to one.

Remember, Blanche DuBois was a blotto and her trip to New Orleans didn't get her anywhere. Nuff said.

St. Patrick's is your lucky day.

CELLULITE
4. The Bumpy. April

June is a badly aspected month for you Cellulites. You tend to be grouchy, cynical, self-serving, petty, stubborn, and bubbly.

But if your name isn't June, you have nothing to worry about. Stand by for jury duty on the 5th through the 18th. The defendant will be heavily armed (thanks to those clumsy new determinate sentencing laws).

These are fine days for the defendant too, especially if he is a Coyote with a Janitor rising.

Remember, you Cellulites, beauty is only skin deep, and there is the rub.

In-laws, the Aggravators, will boost your food bills this month. Be on the lookout for them.

Also, when dining out, be sure to check under the table for looky-loos.

12th and the 14th are your days for shoplifting. Go crazy!

SQUIRREL
5. The Ditzy. May

June is an awfully good month for a whirlwind romance with the president of a small record company.

Watch out for beard rash!

Brush up your wardrobe and smile, darn you, smile.

Arguments about family and homes are settled by a hatchet murder. You Ditzies are notorious for having the last word.

Your personality attracts many Italians because of your innate desire for a well-balanced pizza.

Hygiene is not your long suit, so don't be afraid to jump in the tub around the 24th.

Someone bearing the sign of Dossier, the Ambassador, will interrupt you while you are watching your favorite *I Love Lucy* episode. Don't be afraid to exercise the Squirrel creed, "I can't talk now, I'm washing my hands." That will be sure to get you off the hook.

Your lucky days are St. Vitus and St. Preservus.

EGGPLANT

6. The Thin-Skinned. June

Your Chevrolet rising will be in a beer bar, for all you Eggplants between the 3rd and the 18th. This could bring a mugging and a hangover.

On the 13th a saleslady may make a derogatory remark about your teeth. The best comeback for this insult is to say, "That's okay, they aren't mine."

An old friend is unkind and could involve you in the buying of sandals. No, no, no.

Beware of Princess the Shiksa when she says she wants to have you for dinner. Remember, you're the Eggplant.

Stand by for stardom. You are going to cut a record late this month.

Your lucky numbers are: Area Code 212.

IN-LAWS

7. The Aggravators. July

Your daughter-in-law, the Shiksa, will have problems with her Scientology auditor on the 15th of June. Don't get involved because, as you know, it is an upstart org and you may mess up her case gain.

You Aggravators are going to get your feathers ruffled this month over Concorde landing rights.

There will be a sale on Second Debut at Macy's on the 1st. Don't be afraid to stock up.

You are going shopping for stationery on the last Tuesday of the month. Be choosy and pick out something that enhances your own very special Palmer Method handwriting.

Remember that Adele Hugo, Victor's daughter, was an Aggravator and it was because of her stationery that she got into one heck of a mess.

Your lucky day is any day you don't have to reach for the tomato juice.

PANDA

8. The Cosmetologist. August

Panda, Panda, Panda, this is your month for a very new and charming eyebrow arch. Make sure you get a champion archer because your eyebrows are crucial to your entire look.

You will take a trip to Las Vegas on the weekend of the 16th to see *Wayland and Madam*. But a shuffle at the crap table will constipate you and the trip will probably be for naught.

Your favorite red halter top will get ripped to shreds in a blow-dryer accident. Not to grouse; it could have been your fourteen-karat chain necklace instead.

Your lucky day is any day you don't break a nail.

JANITOR

9. The Slow-Moving. September

You will be wearing your overalls from the 1st to the 8th of June. Make sure that they are either Big Yank or Wrangler. You are going to have a confrontation with the principal on Tuesday the 5th at 2:15 p.m. You will both be interested in the same teacher's aide. The principal will probably pull rank on you, leaving you holding the mop, so to speak. That's okay, there is more than one way to break into a locker.

Since most of you Janitors have Blotto the Drunk rising, and you do long for a holiday, wait until summer school starts and then hop in your truck with some Four Star tequila and a tape deck.

Janitor celebrities with birthdays this month include Nathanael West, Norm Crosby, and Way Bandy.

104

10. The Shiksa. This sign starts whenever you want it to or whenever you finish your makeup, depending on which comes first.

June is the perfect month for you Princesses. Department-store sales galore and a wonderful time to take in all your precious gems for those annual appraisals.

After the 15th men will swarm around you like the facialists at Elizabeth Arden's.

Get your financial status straight toward mid-month. Ask your dad to hike up your yearly allowance.

Toward the end of the month you will come into contact with a Dossier, the Ambassador. He will be tall, handsome, blueblooded, European, and without a cent to his name. Don't let dad find out.

Worst days forecast this month are the day your face breaks out and the day you run out of paper plates.

DOSSIER

11. The Ambassador. November

Your week-at-a-glance diary will be lost in customs on the 23rd. Don't complain. That's how they do things in Argentina. Stay away from the Businessman's Special in the UN commissary. It's a seafood salad and you could pick up a bad case of Sam and Ella.

Your current girlfriend, Miss Aruba, will be the number-one runner-up in the Miss Universe contest. Don't send flowers in Aruba; they are considered bad manners.

You are going to catch a Janitor, the Slow-Moving, trying to infiltrate your offices. Give him what for, but don't tell him who from.

June 31st is the perfect time to patch up any differences you may have with Ethel Merman, but please, whatever you do, don't mention *McHale's Navy*.

Other famous Dossiers include three of the four Modernaires, Lou Brock, and Joan Didion.

12. The Loud and Abrasive. December

On the 14th you are going to tell Rhonda Fleming what you really think of her.

5 FAMILIAR EXPLANATIONS GIVEN TO CLAIMS ADJUSTERS

1. "I was on my way to the barber when I hit a Seville."
2. "I was sure the little old lady was just fooling around when I ran over her and her housedress."
3. "To avoid striking a pedestrian, I pulled into the McDonald's, but he was in my space so I hit him anyway."
4. "The indirect cause of the accident was that I heard Lorraine Day and Leo Durocher were back together."
5. "I had just finished rereading *Elvis, What Happened?* when I rear-ended an El Dorado."

7 HINTS HÉLOISE DIDN'T TAKE SERIOUSLY

1. Wearing day-of-the-week panties as a makeshift hairnet.
2. Short-sheeting a three-layer cake.
3. Using the baby as the theme centerpiece.
4. Using grandpa's denture case as a silent butler.
5. Forcing Foo-Foo to sleep with his mouth open to keep Grandma off the bed.
6. Painting a picture of Leon Spinks on the cookie jar to keep the kids away.
7. Letting a yeast infection rise.

13 QUESTIONS AND ANSWERS FROM TV MAIL CALL

1. Q. You can make me five dollars richer. I have a bet going with my wife that Donna Reed and Horst Buchholz are related. My wife says that Donna's only sister is June Havoc. Who gets the fiver?

A. You're both wrong.

2. Q. My wife is just crazy about Walter Brennan. Can you tell me his shoe size?
   A. 9½ D, but hold on: Mr. Brennan passed on years ago.

3. Q. I heard that Frank Sinatra, Jr., has a famous father.
   A. You heard right. Frank Sinatra, Sr., is also a singer.

4. Q. I watched a movie the other evening and it kept me awake all night. Can you tell me the name of it?
   A. My guess is that it was a Bogdanovich film.

5. Q. I claim they use real people on all the soap operas. My husband claims they're all actors. What do you claim?
   A. I claim you're nuts.

6. Q. My son wants to have plastic surgery on his ears to make him look like Mr. Spock. What do you say? (A no will get you a fiver.)
   A. You haven't told me how old your son is.

7. Q. I would like to get out of the Army on a Section 8. What shows should I watch?
   A. Anything on PBS before 12:00 noon.

8. Q. Somebody told me that Jack Webb got his name because of his feet. Can you verify this?
   A. No.

9. Q. I am unemployed and watch a lot of TV. Will this hurt my job chances?
   A. I don't see how.

10. Q. Question: Is it true that Johnny Carson and Merv Griffin are *not* close personal friends? I say it is.
    A. Then why are you writing me?

11. Q. Why aren't there any commercials on the educational channel? I mean, it's great, but how do they do it?
    A. See above.

12. Q. Isn't that Anita Ekberg in the youngest-child slot on the series *They Lived on Lemp?*
    A. You're half right. It's Phil Ekberg.

13. Q. Was Lassie real or was it just someone in an ape costume? I have five big ones riding on this.
    A. I quit.

19
I CAN NAME THAT TUNE
IN THREE NOTES

3 Ways Bob Dylan Warms Up for a Concert

1. Helping Cher remove her eye makeup.
2. Inviting Joan Baez over for backgammon.
3. Doing chin-ups on his harmonica holder.

6 Things Record Executives Do in Their Spare Time

1. Play fifty-two-card pickup with their backstage passes.
2. Put their Mercedes-Benz up for collateral in a dope deal.
3. Spit-shine their gold records.
4. Try to break into the movie business.
5. Call people "My man."
6. Tell people they knew Linda Ronstadt when she was Rhonda Linstadt!

1 DJ Not Into Polyester

1. Pat Hobby...thinks "leisure suits" are cases lawyers handle in their spare time.

3 Reasons the Beatles Will Never Get Back Together

1. Yoko.
2. Linda.
3. Ringo.

5 Hip Ways to Get Noticed at a Rock Concert

1. Remove all of your clothes and try to sit in with the band.
2. Take ten Quaaludes and lie down in the center aisle.
3. Play, at full volume, a cassette of Hitler's address to the 1936 Olympics.
4. Have an accident in your pants and wear it on your head.
5. Try to slip past the equipment manager dressed as a guitar.

1 Man with a Name Like a Sincere Bathroom Fixture

1. Ernest Tubb.

4 Catch Phrases of Stereo-Component Salesmen

1. "Libra, right?"
2. "I calls 'em as I sees 'em."
3. "Well, you're either into quality or you're not."
4. "Console???!!"

4 Ways to Tell a True Music Lover

1. His wife is wearing a shawl.
2. He keeps his eyes closed even during the intermission.
3. He thinks Save the Whales is a foundation to preserve mature divas.
4. His idea of a good bathroom book is a facsimile manuscript of the Brandenburg Concertos.

8 Things Found in Bruce Springsteen's Overnight Bag

1. A Polaroid of Bruce and his dad in an emergency room with Patti Smith.
2. A preppie reporter from *Rolling Stone*.
3. A dog-eared copy of *How to Increase Your Word Power*.
4. A tank-top organizer from Maxfield Blue.
5. A thank-you note from Ray Kroc.
6. Andy Devine's dialect tapes.
7. An "I'm the Boss" desk plate.
8. Acoustical information on the Grand Canyon.

3 Non-Blacks Named after Precious Stones

1. Perle Mesta.
2. Ruby Keeler.
3. Neil Diamond.

3 People Who Claim to Be Former Pips

1. Garrett Morris.
2. Glenn Ford.
3. Aleksandr Solzhenitsyn

3 Catch Phrases Frequently Used by a Cocktail Pianist

1. "Stop putting my tips in the aquarium, fruit face!"
2. "For the last time, I don't know the words to 'Disco Inferno.' "
3. "Up *your* lazy river, buster!"

6 JOBS FOR THE ROCKETTES ONCE THEY FINALLY CLOSE RADIO CITY MUSIC HALL

1. Bride.
2. Sequin monitor at a Las Vegas sportswear outlet.
3. Alternate companion for George Jessel.
4. Stunt woman for Gloria Vanderbilt.
5. Bunny mother for the June Taylor Dancers.
6. "Scuffy" adjuster for Prudential.

3 POP SINGERS SAMMY DAVIS HASN'T CLAIMED AS A BROTHER

1. The Lennon Sisters.

20
ALL THE NUTS AREN'T IN
THE NUT HOUSE

7 THINGS FOUND IN THE PERSONAL-EFFECTS FILE AT BELLEVUE HOSPITAL

1. Zelda Fitzgerald's toe shoes.
2. A can of Top Coverage hair paint.
3. A backstage pass for *A Tribute to Elvis*.
4. Detailed directions to Montgomery Clift's gravesite.
5. A nametag inscribed "Hi...my name is Mrs. Nobody."
6. One ticket stub from *The Phil Donahue Show*.
7. An ABBA T-shirt.

6 EXCUSES MATCHMAKERS GIVE WHEN THE MATCH GOES ADRIFT

1. "How was I to know he had a birthmark that big?"
2. "She looked like a woman to me."
3. "I told you she was dark-complected."
4. "No, no, no, I said she was in the *road* company of *70 Girls 70*."
5. "Three teeth, so who is needing more?"
6. "You wouldn't say that if you knew how hard underarm hair is to remove."

3 MEDIA PRINCESSES WHO THINK THAT GUCCI IS A SIGN OF THE ZODIAC

1. Britt Ekland.
2. Bianca Jagger
3. Lillian Carter.

4 THINGS A MAN DOES TO LET YOU KNOW THAT HE IS A PREPPIE AT HEART

1. Checks out his crew-neck sweaters to make sure they say, "Made in England."
2. Graciously thanks people when they say, "Boy, do you look Aryan."
3. When you fix him up with a hooker, he asks if she's wellbred.
4. Wears jodhpurs to water the lawn.

6 POPULAR SWEDISH SUICIDES

1. Swallowing a Volvo.
2. Drinking a bottle of Aquavit and flicking your Bic.
3. O.D.-ing on Bergman films.
4. Walking into a crowd of Norwegians.
5. Taking a sitz-bath in battery acid.
6. Washing down lefse with Oil of Olay.

5 WAYS TO SPOT A CIRCUS PERFORMER ON THE STREET

1. There is a snake crawling out of his turtleneck.
2. She needs a shave.
3. They are both wearing the same pair of pants.
4. He's riding the bus bareback.
5. He wears tennis shoes on his hands.

3 OF JOE DON BAKER'S ALTERNATIVE CHOICES FOR FIRST NAME

1. Ray Bob.
2. Jim Bob.
3. Nose Bob.

4 Ways You Let a Friend Take Advantage of You

1. Volunteering your wife to help him with his sexual problems.
2. Lending him your grandmother's fine crystal for his six-year-old's outdoor birthday party.
3. Cosigning for him on a tar-pit scam.
4. Letting him house-sit for you. (He eats a lot and his sister's name is Jo-Jo.)

6 Prerequisites for Working in an Art Gallery

1. A preference for the same sex.
2. The ability to wear loafers with an evening dress.
3. Knowing how to say "Please don't touch" in seven foreign languages.
4. Being able to raise one eyebrow and French-inhale at the same time.
5. Charter membership in the Brad Dourif Fan Club.
6. A willingness to trim beards at a moment's notice.

4 Situations Where You Should Ask for ID

1. When a circus clown pulls you over for speeding.
2. When Larraine Newman poses as a high-fashion model.
3. When your wife says Curly Joe is her kind of man.
4. When your dad starts insisting he was Mahalia Jackson in a former life.

6 THINGS FOUND IN ERNEST HEMINGWAY'S OVERNIGHT BAG

1. Toreador pants.
2. Elephant tranquilizers.
3. An ice pack.
4. A beard gauge.
5. Granddaughter Margaux's eyebrow tweezers.
6. A yellowing *Esquire* article entitled "Genius Is a Sometime Thing."

5 UNCOMMON BUMPER STICKERS

1. Warning, I Break for Halter Tops.
2. No Insurance!!!!
3. If You Can Read This, You Must Have Your Green Card.
4. Yell If You See a Mailbox.
5. Boy, These Nuts are High!

1 PERSON WHO DIDN'T READ *FEAR OF FLYING*

1. Amy Vanderbilt.

5 WAYS ZELDA GOT ON F. SCOTT FITZGERALD'S NERVES

1. She kept after Scott to take her to a bullfight.
2. After Scott would finish a writing project, she would ask with a twinkle in her eye, "Is this the only copy?"

3. She kept bugging him to get her her own special on CBS Radio called *Zelda with a Z.*
4. Whenever he got a rejection slip, she would sing a few bars from "Whoops there goes another rubber tree plant."
5. She wanted to name their Hollywood bungalow "The Dew Drop Inn."

3 OBSCURE LITERARY ANECDOTES

1. OSCAR WILDE
(Fingal O'Flahertie Wills) 1854-1900

Sentenced to two years hard labor at Reading Gaol, Wilde polished his writing style and his sweet tooth. The latter, already well developed before his incarceration, had grown insatiable behind bars. In fact, Wilde existed on little else but cream-filled Napoleons during his entire term at the Gaol. He was known to have bribed the guards and the dessert chef, principally with cigarettes and naughty Greek post cards, to make sure his sweet tooth would never go wanting. One evening, after debauching himself with double orders of strawberries and cream, trifle, and chocolate mousse, Wilde was near faint from overeating and had collapsed, falling headfirst into his toilet pail. A passing guard, seeing the celebrated prisoner's predicament, inquired sarcastically, "Now, Your Lordship, there's no need to be doing that. I'll get you another dessert—but you'll have to take what the rest of us get." Wilde lifted himself out of the muck, tossed his head high, and winked, "Certainly, my good fellow. There's always room for Gaol-O!"

2. BARBARA CARTLAND 1901-

The prolific author of popular romances was in the back seat of her yellow Bentley cruising Bond Street looking for a new wazoo. After passing the same stretch of boutiques for the third time, Harry, Miss Cartland's chauffeur and confidant, pulled the limousine over to the curb, turned around, and asked, "Madame...where is your old wazoo?"

"Old wazoo?" exlaimed Miss Cartland. "If I knew where my old wazoo was, I wouldn't be looking for a new one! Drive on!"

3. WILLIAM SHAKESPEARE 1564-1616

Returning to Stratford after years of success in London, Shakespeare entered the shop of his tailor only to discover the proprietor absent. Hoping to rouse a sleeping apprentice, he called to the rear of the building, but the Bard of Avon soon realized he was alone. Thinking he'd wait for the tailor to return (with the door unlatched, could its keeper be far?), Shakespeare walked to the cutting table and picked up a bolt of cloth to better examine the weave. No sooner had he lifted the fabric when another customer entered, staggering to and fro.

"I'll have my sheets! Have you na' cut them?"

The dramatist, trying to ignore the drunken intruder, did not respond.

"I'll have my sheets! Have you na' cut them?"

Shakespeare did not look up and continued to finger the material.

"You there, Master Snot! You be deaf? I'LL HAVE MY SHEETS! Have you na' cut them?"

The brightest star in all of literature had had enough. Throwing the cloth to the floor, he turned to the sot and exclaimed, "I don't work here."

3 OF THE LONGEST SENTENCES EVER WRITTEN EXCERPTED FROM VERY OBSCURE '40s DETECTIVE NOVELS

From SERVICES RENDERED

1.   I took a gander at the fluff with the slit up her skirt and eyes as big as sapphires in a windstorm, while she held the shiv at my belly, and singsonged a lot of garble about a pretty boy named Ernest, who wore Gardenia cologne, and danced in a colored joint on Central Ave., near Fourth Street in downtown L.A., which wasn't too far from where the Hollywood sign is, overlooking the San Fernando Valley on one side, and dumping out onto Franklin Ave. on the other, and I knew that I

117

didn't have one good reason in the world to be poking my nose into other people's dirty laundry.

From LADY in a TIZZY

2.   Teresa LaSarre held one hand on the wheel, and pushed a pointed-toe alligator pump on the gas pedal real hard, until the palm trees that stood at attention on Highland Ave. started flashing by the windows of the coupe like so many feather fans that a streetwise fan dancer at the height of her career at a clip joint on the wrong side of town would be dizzy from the sight of these tropical delights, but this didn't phase Teresa, who had the brains of a steamed vegetable and a body with so many curves it looked like a traffic jam on Mulholland Drive.

From BLACKMAIL WAS HER GAME

3.   I got a glimpse of the piece in his jacket that hung on his body like a dead fish waiting to be cleaned, just as he seemed to be rubbing his eye where J.P. Brooks, the bigtime industrialist from up Santa Barbara way, had his henchman Charlie the Lump work him over until he started to sing about Brooks' daughter who had been cozy with a two-bit chisler with the tag of Vince, who was seen plenty in places people like him shouldn't be seen in, talking to other smalltime hustlers he should have left alone, and driving a Caddy to the front door of Lucey's on nights when the big muckymucks from Beverly Hills came out ablaze in diamonds and smiles that cost more dough than a dusky sees in a month of Sundays, and the lug said something about his eye.

3 *Playbill* Biographies from the Hit Musical Comedy *Heat Rash*

1. RALPH ADONIS (Simon Thatcher): Mr. Adonis, a native of Parma, Italy, founded Teatro Immigranto five years ago on Ellis Island, where he claims he was "first bitten by the theatri-

cal bug." He was discovered there by the casting director of *The Sicilian Ape* and hired on the spot for the part of Benno the Bodyguard in that movie. Ralph has spent the last three years voluntarily behind bars at Attica State Prison, where he compiled research for his screenplay, *Untitled Prison Movie*, which he describes as a "saga about inmates." Mr. Adonis is married and the father of five or six children. In his spare time (which is precious little for this popular talent) he enjoys hanging out in his tailor-made suits.

2. DEREK MICHAEL-KEATON (Joey LaGazzi): No stranger to New York audiences, having performed in the Ron Reed productions *Mink Breath, There's Always a Spoilsport,* and the all-black version of *Funny Faces of 1975*. A former bath-house manager, swimwear designer, and wrestling coach, Derek says his first love is the theater. When he's not on stage, you'll probably find the multitalented Mr. Michael-Keaton up to his ears in choreography. "Right now, I'm presently at work on a quasi-musical mime one-man show based on the Rolling Stones' single 'When the Whip Comes Down.'" Good luck, Derek, as if you needed any!

3. MILOS MACBETH (Bernie Thomas): Winner of last year's Datsun Drama Award, Mr. Macbeth has had a wide range of experience both on and off stage. He got his big break in the professional theater as personal secretary and valet to Tennessee Williams. His tenure with Mr. Williams soon led to other theatrical "odd jobs" including dresser for Ralph Adonis in the road company of *Rosin Shine*, appointments secretary for Ralph Adonis during the filming of *Towering Bees*, and memo runner for Ralph Adonis' production of *Remember the Ponderosa*. Offstage, New York audiences will recognize Milos as the morning doorman at the Guggenheim Museum.

6 CHEAP QUOTES FOUND IN WEEK-AT-A-GLANCE DIARIES

1. "Today will be boring." —George Sanders

2. "This day's on the house." —F. Scott Fitzgerald
3. "Today is a good day for a cucumber facial." —Cybill Shepherd
4. "Today is not the day I'd like to make it, if some bimbo with a .45 in some bungalow on Hollywood Blvd. starts taking a shine to snuffing out a peeper who's just nickel-and-diming it through life." —Boston Blackie
5. "Today is a good day to score penicillin." —Idi Amin
6. "Today is a good day to lounge around." —Maxfield Parrish

8 SELF-HELP BOOKS IN SEARCH OF PUBLISHERS

1. *Tying Your Own Shoes.*
2. *Better Off Dead.*
3. *God Was Just Pulling Your Leg.*
4. *NUTS Is a Four-Letter Word.*
5. *Mental Health Isn't for Everyone.*
6. *Ah, Ah, Ah, Don't Touch That Wrist.*
7. *Schizo and Other Phrenics.*
8. *Hate Yourself to Suicide.*

5 VICTORIAN NOVELS OVERLOOKED BY THE *NEW YORK TIMES BOOK REVIEW*

1. *Withering Tights.*
2. *Love Hankie.*
3. *Hold My Lips.*
4. *Rogue, Rogue, Rogue Your Boat.*
5. *For the Love of Leroy.*

6 WANT ADS YOU ARE LIKELY TO FIND IN AN EAST COAST LITERARY MAGAZINE

1. Wanted: Handwriting to analyze. We've already done ours.

2. Wanted: Small businessmen—4'11'' to 5'1''. Increase profits and height.
3. Book Plates. Service for twelve. Barely used.
4. Partner wanted to share henna chores. Applied weekly. Will be happy to rinse.
5. Moving to Cleveland. Good luck.
6. Rare Photos of Elvis and Jean Paul Sartre together at famous Long Island jam. $1.00 Postage Paid.

3 EXCERPTS FROM "REVEALING" BIOGRAPHIES

1. AN EXCERPT FROM THE FAMED LIZETTE NORMAND'S SOON-TO-BE-PUBLISHED AUTOBIOGRAPHY, *CAVIAR AND BUGATTIS*

September 11, 1939

I had just finished wrapping up work on the picture, *The Enchanted Stutz*, which featured yours truly in the lead, and my supporting players were Mischa Auer, Leslie Howard, and Judy Canova. My designer, Fabian of Burbank, had whipped up tons of fabulous gowns for me, in all the most dazzling shades of pink. One in particular, a chiffon number with dolman sleeves, just cried for me to wear it. Since the studio always let me keep my wardrobe, I decided the night that the film wrapped to put on the rose dolman, and of course some French embroidered underthings, and yes, some jewelry, and powder and other girlish things, and I jumped into my Bugatti and drove to the Trocadero Club to celebrate the picture.

Well, little did I know as I cruised Sunset Boulevard, heading toward the Trock, what an evening was in store.

I entered the club, and simply everyone was there, whooping it up: Clark Cable; George Bernard Shaw; Dottie Parker, out from the East; William Faulkner; Winston Churchill; F. Scott Fitzgerald; Lupe Velez; Frances Farmer; and John Belushi. Everyone was having a heck of a time. I was greeted at the door by Mike Romanoff, who had been a best man at one of my weddings. I can't remember which one, but I remember Mike looking simply fabulous in a tux that Fabian had designed for him. Mike sat me at the best table, and I barely got settled, when F. Scott came up to me, with a bottle of Scotch in one hand and a copy of Ernest Hemingway's royalty check in the other. Scott took one look at my dress, slapped his knee, and yelled, "Fabian, right?" and started laughing like a hyena. I laughed, too. It was all terribly gay. Then Scott told me about a problem he had with Fabian when he had commissioned him to make a cashmere overcoat with a portable bar in the lining. They had a falling-out over the pockets and that's when Scott said, "Fabian and I didn't ruin each other, we ruined ourselves." That quote is sometimes thought to pertain to Scott's relationship with Zelda, but he said it to me, and I know he was talking about Fabian of Burbank and the coat incident. Just then, Lupe Velez, that Mexican spitfire, came to the table and Scott sauntered off. Lupe was particularly P.O.'d that evening because her then husband, Johnny Weismuller, had thrown her in the enchilada-shaped swimming pool earlier in the day. That crazy Latin was still fuming about it. She called Weissmuller everything from a whitey hombre to a cucaracha, until Dick Powell got her to get in the conga line. Dancing is the only thing that calms some Latins down.

Then Winston Churchill came up to the table and joined me for some champagne. We talked about my last picture. We were having a splendid time until a blonde came up to Winston and said, "Why, Winston, you're drunk." Winston turned to her and scowled, "That's right, madame. I'm drunk and you're ugly, but tomorrow I'll be sober." The blonde went too, too crazy, and I tried to calm them both down by some smalltalk about Fabian of Burbank. We all had a good laugh. William Faulkner came by our table, and Winston stuck his foot out and tripped the writer, at which time Bill Faulkner rose to his feet and said, "If I have to choose between pain and nothing, I would rather take pain." With that he limped off.

The evening was going great guns until Frances Farmer came in on the arm of John Belushi. Belushi was miffed because someone had mistaken him for Lou Costello, and he was also peeved that the band wouldn't let him sit in with them, and Frances Farmer was screeching about some traffic violation. But I saved the day by bringing them into a conversation about Fabian of Burbank, and they all had a good laugh. Frances was trying to balance a couple of highball glasses on top of her head, gay madcap that she was, and that's when Dorothy Parker strolled over to the table and said, "Men don't make passes at girls who wear glasses." Dotty was always good for a laugh. What a sparkling evening it was. I looked at my watch and it was nearly two a.m., and I had a nine-a.m. fitting schedule with Fabian the next morning. I said my goodbyes and left the Trocadero Club and floated to the parking lot to pick up my Bugatti. A small Negro boy was the parking-lot attendant that evening, and he fetched my car. He said, "I'm really tired," and rubbed his little eyes as he handed me my keys. I said, "It is two a.m. What time do you get off work?" He smiled at me and said he was off at two, and then he said, "Free at last! Free at last! Great God Almighty, I'm free at last!"

I drove home that evening having had a marvelous time.

2. AN EXCERPT FROM FAMED MOTION-PICTURE STAR MONTY DESMOND'S SOON-TO-BE PUBLISHED BIOGRAPHY, *THE AWFUL AWFUL THINGS I'VE DONE*

Twilight, 1960

I had just returned from a trip to the South Seas when I docked my yacht in a Los Angeles harbor. My beautiful boat, the *Chuga Chuga*, which means "dirty" in Spanish, had always been an enormous source of pleasure to me. She was the only lady in my life that I could really control, with the exception of a little waitress I once had in Singapore; but more about that later on. It was the twenty-first of June and I had received a cable in Tahiti that I was wanted back in the States for two reasons. The first was that I had landed that role of Rollo in the soon-to-be-filmed picture *Rollo Lands on Anzio Beach*. The second reason for my return was a hearing in the Santa Monica Courthouse. I was once again accused of fathering a child. The evidence was not stacked in my favor. I remember saying to Lupita Torrez, my then wife, "If I had really been as sexually active as people say I am, I wouldn't have much time left to drink." Lupita had looked at me curiously because she never did understand English. Anyway, back to court I went. A young dancer with breasts that stood at attention was making the accusations this time around. I had fought my battles in the Santa Monica courtrooms on the same charges fifty-one times from 1941 to 1956. I never won a single case. Hollywood had labled me "the cad." I was never one to run away from a fight, and no matter how black the prospects looked, I went to this trial with my head held high. I drank a fifth of bourbon, waxed my mustache, and entered the courtroom. Lila Lamont, the mother in question, was sitting with her attorney, Floyd Beal, as I entered. "Oh no," I said upon seeing Floyd Beal. Right then and there I thought my goose was cooked. He was one of the most famous trial lawyers in the country.

The trial went on for weeks and my picture was pasted across every tabloid in the country; but just when it looked the worst for me, something happened that altered the case completely. Mysteriously, Lila Lamont came forward and admitted that the whole thing had been a sham. It seemed she knew the judge would make a decision in her favor and it turns out that the fun all went out of it for her. She suddenly changed her story and said that Gable was the real father. The case was thrown out.

I went home to my house on Mulholland Drive and celebrated my first triumph over the courts. I felt like a million bucks. I threw a bash that evening, and all my closest chums were there. We all drank and carried on for hours until disaster struck again. My wife Lupita put a damper on the evening by taking a lethal dose of barbituates and lay stone dead on the floor of our bedroom. She was discovered by my loyal houseboy, Emil.

The entire next day I was really in a slump, until my old friend Errol Flynn stopped by to cheer me up. Errol and I went back a long way. We were about as close as men can get without being fairies about the whole thing. Errol pointed out that life could be tough, but what the hell. He made me see the light. He even agreed to lend me a copy of Thomas DeQuincey's *Confessions of an English Opium Eater*. That cheered me up immensely. Soon afterward I was in the pink again. I started filming *Rollo Lands on Anzio Beach*, and fell madly in love with

124

my costar, Carmen Casalez. We married before the filming was completed. The marriage ended abruptly when I found out she both spoke and understood English. I never liked a woman I could communicate with.

3. AN EXCERPT FROM FAMED STAR MAY ST. FAY'S SOON-TO-BE-PUBLISHED AUTOBIOGRAPHY, *DON'T LET THE BEDBUGS BITE*

September, 1945

I remember very vividly the first day I met Louie B., the studio patriarch. I had just come to MGM from Republic, where I had gotten a lot of attention in my last picture, *His Right-Hand Man*. I was making a lot of women's pictures, usually playing the career girl who comes on strong, but deep down has mush for a heart. I walked into Louie B.'s office to protest what I felt had been a major crime being perpetrated against me. The studio wrote it into my contract that I could never wear anything but a tailored suit in any given film, whether it was a period piece, a western, or what-have-you. I strolled up to Mr. Mayer and said, "Papa..." (That's what everybody called him.) I said, "Papa, what's all this rot about a navy gob tailored suit. I may not be a glamorpuss like some of the dames on this lot, but I would like to have a chance once in a while to wear a smart feminine frock, or slacks or what-have-you, too." Mr. Mayer was toking on a cigar, staring right at me, and he did not say a word. Finally he broke the silence with, "Honey, you've got spunk. I won't change the wording in the contract, but if you do some benefits for the GI's and keep your nose clean, I'll see to it personally that in your next picture you get a behind-a-dressing-screen silhouette of you changing your clothes, and if that don't change your image, I don't know what will."

I was aghast. I had come to slay the dragon and walked away with a little something to show for it.

My second picture at the studio was a lulu. It was *Four Men and a Rather Mannish Woman*. I played the lead—a zany, screwball businesswoman with a weakness for taxis. My costars were Albert Finney, Albert Dekker, Albert Schweitzer, and Albert DiSalvo. I got my dressing-room-screen scene in that film and every other one I ever did at MGM.

Life magazine did a cover story on me as the only woman who singlehandedly did more for a tailored mannish forties suit since who knows when, or what-have-you.

When I received my special Oscar in 1949 for being the best darned typist/actress in films, I literally cried all the way to the podium. To think that they were honoring me, May St. Fay, and in my heart I knew that Louie B. was right. Everybody likes a gal with spunk.

22
THEOLOGY

4 Ways to Get a Jehovah's Witness off Your Back

1. Ask them to name ten celebrities who are Jehovah's Witnesses.
2. Ask them if they'll take a two-party check.
3. Show them the Patti D'Arbanville spread in *Hombre*.
4. Hike your dress up and ask them if they'd like to see your "itchings."

10 Ways Parish Priests Raise Extra Money

1. Converting pagan babies.
2. Selling inside information to *True Confessions*.
3. Dealing baccarat at the bingo hall.
4. Making book on the Cardinals.
5. Introducing chicken hawks to their catechism classes.
6. Collecting ten percent on every kid they send to Boys' Town.
7. Playing Friar Tuck at the Community Theater.
8. Selling their old alpaca sweater collection to Ricardo Montalban.
9. Cornering the market on Knights of Columbus scatter pins.
10. Raffling off their old housekeepers.

6 Patron Saints Removed from the Calendar

1. St. Jalapeno, patron saint of Mexican food.
2. St. Alphonso Bedoya, patron saint of stinking badges.
3. St. Malden, patron saint of traveler's checks.
4. St. Pinter, patron saint of lost pauses.
5. St. John of Cassavetes, patron saint of self-indulgence.
6. St. Rose of Marie, patron saint of talk shows.

4 Requirements Needed to Join the Jesuits

1. The ability to distinguish Latin from Ladino.
2. Memorizing at least three limericks that rhyme with St. Ignatius.
3. The good sense to stay away from Christian Brothers wine-tasting parties.
4. Knowing what goes well with a rope sash.

5 Snappy Retorts to Discourage an Overzealous Hare Krishna

1. "Sorry, I don't talk to skinheads."
2. "If you don't buzz off, I'll make you eat white bread."
3. "Spare change?"
4. "Who does your sheets?"
5. "Didn't I see you in *Gunga Din?*"

3 Ways the Pope Spends His Day Off

1. He takes a stroll down the Via Veneto saying, "Now, that's Italian!"
2. He enjoys a Campari and holy water on the rocks.
3. He calls St. Louis long-distance to see how the Cardinals are doing.